NAVIGATING THE CHALLENGES OF ENTREPRENEURSHIP

Empowering Strategies for Success

Michelle Hauger

Contents

Introduction

The interplay between ideas, economies, and progress has made innovation and entrepreneurship inseparable in today's global landscape. Governments worldwide are awakening to the realization that nurturing a nation's economy and fostering sustainable growth necessitates fostering a culture of out-of-the-box thinking and continuous development of groundbreaking products and services. Traditional approaches to business that were once deemed reliable can no longer guarantee future economic triumphs.

In response to this inevitable shift, certain governments are reevaluating the approach to educating the younger generation, integrating creative thinking and innovation into their national curriculum. Similarly, there is a significant emphasis on equipping future entrepreneurs with essential skills by incorporating entrepreneurship elements into the educational system, particularly at the tertiary level. Several nations have even taken this initiative further by introducing entrepreneurship education at elementary schools, fostering a mindset for future entrepreneurial endeavors as students grow older.

In contrast to the conventional career paths of the past, such as becoming a doctor, lawyer, or fighter pilot, being an entrepreneur has become the preferred choice for the new generation. Recent studies have revealed that entrepreneurship, especially in computer science and e-commerce, is a highly desirable and trendy career path among young individuals. This marked a noteworthy shift from earlier perceptions when entrepreneurship was often associated with stigma and viewed as a fallback for those unable to secure stable government jobs. Previously, individuals who pursued entrepreneurship were subjected to ridicule and social exclusion from their peers.

With the changing times, the perception of entrepreneurship has experienced a notable shift. It is now recognized as a credible and captivating career option, offering opportunities for personal fulfillment and financial prosperity. The younger generation is increasingly enticed by the prospect of establishing their ventures, developing groundbreaking products and services, and leaving a positive imprint on society.

With the evolving perception of entrepreneurship and its acknowledged capacity for job creation, the field of entrepreneurship studies has expanded significantly. Numerous tertiary institutions now provide courses in entrepreneurship and innovation to cater to the increasing demand. Moreover, the term "entrepreneurship" has transformed into various variations, including netpreneur, biotechpreneur, technopreneur, and multipreneur, reflecting the dynamic nature of the business landscape.

In light of these shifts, redefining or refining the concept of entrepreneurship to align with the demands of the 21st century is imperative. As highlighted by Bygrave and Hofer (1991), "Good science requires good definitions." With a precise definition of entrepreneurship, policymakers can devise effective programs to foster entrepreneurship within their communities and organizations.

In this comprehensive guide, we will venture into entrepreneurship, offering valuable perspectives on its essence, the requisites for entrepreneurial success, and the prevalent problems and challenges entrepreneurs often encounter. We will delve into the fundamental qualities and skills that set successful entrepreneurs apart and look at practical solutions for overcoming typical roadblocks. Readers will have an inclusive understanding of the entrepreneurial world by the end of this book and will be outfitted with the skills they need to be successful in this exciting, rapidly evolving industry.

SERIES ONE
INTRODUCTION TO
ENTREPRENEURSHIP

The concept of entrepreneurship encompasses diverse interpretations, and its significance has evolved throughout history. While commonly associated with initiating one's business, economists widely concur that it transcends mere business creation.

The term "entrepreneur" finds its roots in the French word "entrepreneur," which translates to "to embark on." Within the business context, it denotes the act of launching a venture. However, being an entrepreneur encompasses more than mere business initiation. It entails organizing, managing, and assuming the associated risks to generate profit or attain success.

Moreover, an entrepreneur can be recognized as someone strongly inclined to catalyze change. These individuals are motivated to explore novel opportunities, challenge established norms, and transform innovative ideas into reality. Entrepreneurship transcends conventional business ventures and extends to diverse spheres, encompassing social entrepreneurship. In this realm, individuals establish enterprises to address social or environmental concerns.

Furthermore, entrepreneurship can be perceived as a mindset or an approach to work. It encapsulates attributes such as creativity, resilience, adaptability, and a willingness to undertake calculated risks. An entrepreneur can also be an individual aspiring to work independently, seeking autonomy and the chance to carve their professional trajectory.

An entrepreneur is a remarkable individual who defies all odds and combines various factors of production, including land, labor, and capital while demonstrating initiative and assuming the risks and uncertainties inherent in business. Regarded as distinct, an entrepreneur fulfills a crucial role as one of the factors of production. "Land" refers to natural resources bestowed by nature in a specific location, contributing to production.

Labor encompasses all human contributions, both physical and mental, that facilitate wealth creation through production. Capital, on the other hand, pertains to all man-made tools and resources utilized to enhance wealth creation further. Each of these factors receives its corresponding reward, such as rent for land, wages/salaries for labor, and interest for capital. An entrepreneur skillfully combines all these factors, as mentioned earlier, to ensure the attainment of their ultimate reward, profit, without compromising any element. Entrepreneurship revolves around an individual's capacity to initiate innovative ideas that not only benefit society but possess the potential to withstand the challenges of the ever-evolving business landscape.

As a business manager, risk taker, decision maker, and overall organizer, the entrepreneur has yet to maximize profit within their business successfully. They are crucial in coordinating the various production factors, ensuring their enterprise's success. With the entrepreneur, the other factors of production would be effectively utilized and harnessed to their fullest potential.

Entrepreneurship presents abundant prospects for success but offers its fair share of challenges. Achieving success as an entrepreneur necessitates possessing a well-defined vision, exceptional leadership abilities, and adaptability in the face of evolving circumstances. Furthermore, entrepreneurs must exhibit a robust work ethic, a willingness to undertake calculated risks, and an unwavering dedication to continuous learning and personal growth. Despite embodying these qualities, entrepreneurs inevitably encounter challenges on their path to success.

Entrepreneurship vs. Small Business

The terms 'entrepreneur' and 'small business' are often used interchangeably, indicating similarity. However, while they share commonalities, notable distinctions exist between an entrepreneurial venture and a small business. An entrepreneurial experience is quite different from a small business in the following ways:

1. Innovation

This is the essence of entrepreneurship, empowering resources to generate wealth. Entrepreneurship often involves profound innovation that goes beyond the scope of a typical small business.

2. Risk

Risk is typically inherent in an entrepreneurial venture, as it is crucial. Without substantial risk, accompanied by the allure of potential profits, numerous entrepreneurs would forego pursuing the idea, thereby eliminating the opportunity.

3. Amount of wealth creation

A thriving entrepreneurial venture yields significant wealth, often surpassing several million dollars in profits, rather than solely generating an income stream that replaces traditional employment.

4. Rapid Wealth Creation

While a prosperous small business can accumulate considerable profits over its lifespan, entrepreneurs often experience swift and accelerated wealth creation, sometimes within just five years. Moreover, the nature of their business pursuits sets them apart, primarily driven by innovation. Innovation serves as a critical factor that entrepreneurs heavily rely on, and its significance can be emphasized in the following ways:

- New organization
- New products

- New markets
- New production methods

When innovation leads to the emergence of new demand, it becomes a catalyst for wealth creation. From this perspective, the role of the entrepreneur can be briefly described as the skillful integration of diverse factors in a creative manner to deliver value to customers. The objective is to ensure that this value exceeds the costs associated with the input factors, thus generating higher returns on investment.

The key distinctions between entrepreneurship and small business lie in the level of risk undertaken and the approach to growth and success. Entrepreneurs embrace risk and strive for immediate and potentially significant returns, propelling themselves with urgency. In contrast, small businesses often begin on a smaller scale, with less risk involved, and gradually build income and success over time through meticulous and controlled planning.

Traits Of A Successful Entrepreneur

Are you curious about the disparity between success and failure among individuals? The key might lie in their unique set of traits and characteristics. Do you exhibit these qualities?

The business landscape has experienced transformative shifts fueled by technological advancements like computers, the internet, and mobile devices. Yet, the foundational traits for business success have roots in earlier generations. Before venturing into entrepreneurship, assessing if you possess the essential qualities required to thrive in the business world is crucial.

Each day, countless individuals worldwide seek an opportunity to become self-employed and establish a thriving home-based business. The options are seemingly limitless, ranging from affiliate marketing, network marketing (MLM), direct sales, eBay businesses information marketing, and more. However, despite the widespread interest in entrepreneurship, only a select few translate their aspirations into action and attain true success.

The lack of the essential trio known as the 3 D's: desire, drive, and decisiveness, is the main reason for this difference. Successful businesspeople have regularly exhibited these traits throughout history. Their unwavering passion compels them to revolutionize or instigate positive transformations within their respective domains. They possess a proactive approach to decision-making, fearlessly embracing calculated risks and navigating challenging choices. Moreover, they are fueled by an unrelenting drive that propels them to persistently pursue their vision, undeterred by any impediments encountered along the way.

Entrepreneurship encompasses more than a mere idea; it demands adopting an apt mindset and cultivating specific traits to transform that idea into a triumphant reality. Flourishing entrepreneurs aren't solely born with these attributes; instead, they acquire and hone the skills and qualities imperative for triumph in business. Let us delve into additional vital traits of a prosperous entrepreneur, pivotal for materializing ideas into tangible achievements.

1. Entrepreneurs Act Amidst Any Conditions

Prosperous entrepreneurs take decisive action regardless of the prevailing conditions they encounter. They grasp the reality that flawless conditions are elusive in the business realm. They comprehend that timing and circumstances can swiftly shift, and the entrepreneurial landscape constantly evolves. Hence, they proactively shape their events, adapting their strategies to align with the present conditions and circumstances.

Entrepreneurial success stems from the recognition that perfection is elusive in business. Instead of waiting for ideal conditions, successful entrepreneurs prioritize action and strive for progress, irrespective of their obstacles. They understand that waiting for the perfect moment may lead to missed opportunities, as they may never materialize. Thus, they embrace a proactive approach, seizing every chance to advance toward their goals.

Successful entrepreneurs endure and thrive in adverse circumstances, employing ingenuity and resourcefulness to overcome challenges. They perceive obstacles as chances for personal development and seize opportunities to learn and grow. By leveraging these experiences, they fortify their resilience and emerge stronger than before.

Take, for instance, the case of Sara Blakely, the visionary behind Spanx. Blakely encountered hurdles and setbacks at the outset of her entrepreneurial journey, such as financial constraints and investor rejections. Nonetheless, she persisted with unwavering determination. Leveraging her resourcefulness and creativity, she ingeniously devised alternative approaches to surmount these challenges. In a testament to her perseverance, she drafted the patent for her product when legal assistance proved unaffordable. Spanx is a billion-dollar enterprise, and Blakely stands tall as a triumphant entrepreneur.

2. Goal-Driven and Productive

Thriving entrepreneurs are proactive and driven by meticulous planning and production. They are adept at setting clear objectives and possess a crystal-clear vision of their destination. They craft robust strategic plans that comprehensively outline the "how," "when," "why," and "what" of their business endeavors.

However, accomplished entrepreneurs avoid becoming overly fixated on the intricacies of the plan. They comprehend that unexpected hurdles and challenges can arise, necessitating their course of action adjustments. As a result, they maintain flexibility and adaptability, consistently prioritizing the desired outcome and the broader perspective.

Furthermore, successful entrepreneurs consistently evaluate the advancement of their business plan to verify their alignment with goals. They recognize the significance of monitoring outcomes and overseeing their business's progress. Employing various metrics and key performance indicators (KPIs), they assess the efficacy of their plan and implement requisite modifications for enhancing business performance.

3. Self-investment

Successful entrepreneurs prioritize self-investment as a crucial factor in their achievements. They understand that personal growth is continuous and aspire to enhance all aspects of their existence. While formal education holds significance, they acknowledge that authentic learning occurs beyond the confines of a classroom. They actively pursue knowledge from diverse outlets such as books, videos, and mentors.

Experienced mentors are pivotal in nurturing the growth of triumphant entrepreneurs. They actively pursue mentors who have already attained the desired outcomes, aiming to gain wisdom from their experiences. These mentors offer priceless insights and counsel on various aspects, from strategic planning to efficient execution.

Prospective entrepreneurs prioritize investing in personal growth and development besides seeking mentors. They read books, attend seminars and conferences, and take courses to broaden their knowledge and enhance their skills. They remain vigilant for novel ideas and diverse perspectives that can contribute to their continual growth and advancement.

Prioritizing personal development entails tending to both physical and mental well-being. Flourishing entrepreneurs grasp the significance of upholding a healthy lifestyle, making exercise, nutrition, and stress management integral to their daily regimen. They comprehend that a sound body and mind are imperative for optimal performance and enduring triumph.

In essence, accomplished entrepreneurs comprehend that self-investment is an ongoing voyage of perpetual growth and development rather than an isolated occurrence. Through a ceaseless pursuit of new knowledge and experiences, they proactively remain ahead of the game, effectively attaining their objectives.

4. Resourcefulness is their defining trait.

Driven by their passion, entrepreneurs showcase two notable facets of resourcefulness that distinguish them from the rest. Firstly, when faced with unfamiliar tasks, they educate themselves or seek capable individuals to handle them. They fearlessly seek assistance and undertake the necessary measures to acquire essential skills or knowledge. Secondly, they exhibit persistence and patience when facing obstacles on their journey. They perceive challenges as chances for growth and actively craft solutions.

They understand that obstacles are merely opportunities for creating, discovering, and implementing solutions. Resourcefulness, a vital characteristic, empowers entrepreneurs to surmount challenges and maintain an unwavering focus on their objectives. They remain vigilant for novel resources, tools, and approaches to propel their business forward. Whether it involves discovering a fresh supplier, recruiting a new team member, or acquiring a new skill, successful entrepreneurs demonstrate resourcefulness in every facet of their business.

5. They are productive action-takers.

Productive action-taking is a hallmark of accomplished entrepreneurs. What sets them apart is their adeptness at focusing on essential tasks, eschewing non-essential activities or busy work. They diligently prioritize their daily, weekly, and monthly schedules, ensuring they promptly and efficiently tackle crucial tasks.

They ensure their goals and objectives align with their long-term vision to maintain productivity. These aspirations are then subdivided into smaller, attainable tasks they consistently pursue. They exhibit no reluctance in delegating tasks to those better suited for them and perpetually strive to enhance their efficiency and effectiveness.

Productive entrepreneurs grasp the finite nature of time and employ tools and techniques to wield it prudently. They establish dedicated periods for email management, sidestep distractions during work hours, and allocate time for self-care activities like exercise and relaxation. These practices enable them to sustain energy and unwavering concentration throughout the day.

Alongside productivity, accomplished entrepreneurs prioritize action-taking. They comprehend that success encompasses more than just possessing brilliant ideas or plans; it requires their implementation. They fearlessly embrace risks and mistakes, perceiving them as invaluable learning opportunities for growth and enhancement.

They understand that failure is not the end but a necessary step toward achievement. They view failures as excellent learning opportunities, and they modify their strategy accordingly rather than getting demoralized by them. They are willing to pivot their design or make necessary plan adjustments to attain their goals.

Productive action-taking is crucial for thriving entrepreneurs. They adeptly prioritize their time and tasks, ensuring continual advancement toward their goals. Fearless in their pursuit, they embrace risks and accept that mistakes are stepping stones on their journey.

Advantages And Disadvantages Of Being An Entrepreneur

Embarking on the entrepreneurial path and pursuing self-employment can be an immensely gratifying career, often the epitome of one's aspirations. Although not devoid of risks and challenges, this journey transcends the confines of a typical 9-5 job, offering many advantages. Let us delve into entrepreneurs' everyday adversities and the compelling long-term benefits that render this career choice alluring.

Advantages of Being an Entrepreneur

- Freedom and Autonomy

Entrepreneurship bestows one of its most significant rewards: freedom and autonomy. By embarking on this path, you seize the power to shape your destiny. Liberated from the confines of a 9-to-5 job and unhindered by another's vision, you can make autonomous decisions, set personal goals, and define success on your terms.

- Pursuing Your Passion

Entrepreneurship grants you the avenue to transform your passion into a gratifying career. It presents the opportunity to construct a business centered around what ignites your spirit. Whether it revolves around a product or service you deeply believe in, or a cause that fuels your enthusiasm, entrepreneurship empowers you to harmonize your work with your core values, fostering a profound sense of purpose and contentment.

- Creativity and Innovation

Entrepreneurship serves as a fertile ground for creativity and innovation. As an entrepreneur, you are perpetually spurred to transcend conventional thinking, discover unconventional solutions, and redefine the limits of possibility. Unrestrained by restrictions, you can delve into uncharted territory, test diverse methodologies, and manifest your imaginative vision into reality.

- Financial Potential

Entrepreneurship presents an avenue for substantial financial rewards, although not guaranteed. As an entrepreneur, you possess the potential to establish a business that yields considerable profits and wealth. Unfettered by fixed salaries or promotion hierarchies, you can forge a venture that offers financial security and the prospect of creating intergenerational prosperity.

- Personal Growth and Learning

Entrepreneurship is an enduring voyage of personal growth and learning. It propels you beyond your comfort zone, tests your boundaries, and fosters individual development. As you navigate the multifaceted realms of business ownership, you acquire new skills, amass invaluable experience, and cultivate a resilient mindset that transcends every facet of your existence.

Disadvantages of Being an Entrepreneur

- Work-Life Balance

Achieving work-life balance poses a noteworthy challenge in the realm of entrepreneurship. The demands of this path often necessitate extensive time and effort, leading to lengthy work hours, personal sacrifices, and a persistent sense of being tethered to your business. Successfully harmonizing emotional well-being, relationships, and professional obligations becomes a delicate art of mindful allocation and conscious prioritization.

- Uncertainty and Risk

Entrepreneurs encounter a fundamental challenge in the form of inherent uncertainty and risk that accompanies starting and operating a business. Success is never guaranteed, and the prospect of failure must be confronted. Achieving success as an entrepreneur requires accepting uncertainty, making difficult decisions based on scant knowledge, and persevering in the face of setbacks.

- Loneliness and Isolation

The entrepreneurial expedition can often induce feelings of solitude. As an entrepreneur, you may confront challenges and make crucial decisions in solitude. This sense of isolation can exact a toll on your mental and emotional well-being, especially during moments of uncertainty or when confronted with setbacks.

Navigating the entrepreneurial realm often necessitates forfeiting personal connections and social interactions. The demands of a business building tend to engulf substantial time and energy, leaving little space for socializing or nurturing a robust support network. It is commonplace for entrepreneurs to devote themselves wholeheartedly to their ventures, toiling during late nights, weekends, and even holidays.

- Financial Instability

Entrepreneurship, particularly in its initial stages, often entails financial instability. Cash flow issues can arise, and it might take some time before your company starts to profit. As an entrepreneur, you might need to put money into your business, get a loan, or look for outside investors to keep it going. Navigating the financial rollercoaster can induce stress, necessitating meticulous financial planning and unwavering resilience.

- Work-Life Imbalance

Entrepreneurs frequently find themselves deeply engrossed in their work, dedicating substantial hours to building and expanding their businesses. Striving for a harmonious work-life balance becomes formidable, demanding intentional actions and professional time management.

Embarking on the entrepreneurial path is an exhilarating and arduous undertaking, presenting various advantages and disadvantages. Although the journey may demand tremendous effort, the rewards can be immeasurable. By confronting challenges with determination and harnessing the benefits of autonomy, growth, creativity, financial potential, and personal fulfillment, entrepreneurs have the chance to carve their trail and establish a purposeful legacy.

How To Assess Your Suitability For Entrepreneurship

Embarking on the entrepreneurial journey is an invigorating choice that warrants thoughtful deliberation. While entrepreneurship presents abundant prospects and rewards, evaluating its congruence with your aspirations, abilities, and disposition is crucial. You can attain clarity and arrive at an informed decision by delving into your motivations, scrutinizing your personality traits, gauging your risk tolerance, and assessing your skills and resources. The following pivotal factors will assist in discerning if entrepreneurship aligns with your path ahead:

Understanding Your Motivations

1. Passion and Purpose

Understand your passions and ascertain their potential for being transformed into a business concept. Inquire within: What propels me? What genuinely ignites my passion? Entrepreneurship flourishes when rooted in a profound sense of purpose, serving as the driving force to surmount hurdles and maintain motivation during challenging moments.

2. Autonomy and Independence

Understand the significance of autonomy and independence in your life. Do you feel at ease making decisions without depending on others? Entrepreneurs relish the freedom to forge their path and assume complete accountability for their choices. Entrepreneurship may resonate with you if you yearn for the autonomy to shape your destiny and possess a strong inclination towards self-guidance.

3. Desire for Impact

Evaluate your yearning to effect a substantial impact. Are you motivated to instigate change and leave an enduring legacy? Entrepreneurship empowers individuals to shape industries, address challenges, and contribute to society in distinctive ways. Entrepreneurship can serve as the platform to manifest your aspirations if you are resolute in making a difference and propelling positive transformation.

Assessing Your Personality Traits

1. Risk Tolerance

Evaluate your comfort level with risk-taking. Entrepreneurship inherently entails uncertainty, and your tolerance for risk plays a pivotal role in navigating challenges. Reflect on whether you are open to stepping beyond your comfort zone, making decisions amidst limited information, and embracing ambiguity. While calculated risks are integral to entrepreneurship, gauging your preparedness to confront the unknown is crucial.

2. Resilience and Perseverance

Assess your resilience and capacity to rebound from failures and setbacks. Entrepreneurship demands a steadfast spirit, as obstacles and hurdles frequently accompany it. Reflect on whether you possess the mindset to glean lessons from failures, adjust to evolving circumstances, and forge ahead. Resilience is a vital attribute that empowers entrepreneurs to surmount challenges and maintain an unwavering dedication to their vision.

3. Adaptability and Flexibility

Evaluate your adaptability and flexibility amidst uncertainty and shifting market dynamics. Entrepreneurship necessitates the capacity to pivot, refine strategies, and seize new prospects. Reflect on your openness to change and perpetual learning and growth. Embracing adaptability empowers entrepreneurs to flourish in dynamic landscapes and leverage emerging trends.

Evaluating Skills and Resources

1. Entrepreneurial Skills

Identify the critical skills required for entrepreneurship, such as creativity, problem-solving, communication, leadership, and financial literacy. Evaluate your proficiency in these areas and your willingness to invest in their further development. By acknowledging your strengths and areas for growth, you can better determine your preparedness for the entrepreneurial journey.

2. Network and Support

Consider the quality of your network and the presence of a support system. While entrepreneurship can be a solitary endeavor, having mentors, advisors, and a community of like-minded individuals can offer guidance, motivation, and valuable connections. Assess the availability of such a support system or your willingness to seek and cultivate it proactively.

3. Financial Resources

Evaluate your financial resources and situation. Entrepreneurship often requires financial investment, whether it be through personal savings, loans, or securing investors. Assess your access to capital and determine if you can support yourself during your business's initial stages. It is crucial to understand your financial resources and how they could affect your personal and professional life.

4. Time Commitment

Consider the time commitment necessary for entrepreneurship. Building and managing a business often requires long hours, sacrifices, and unwavering dedication. Evaluate your current commitments and obligations, such as family responsibilities or other professional engagements. Reflect on whether you are willing to prioritize and dedicate ample time to your entrepreneurial endeavor.

Determining if entrepreneurship is your path requires a comprehensive self-assessment of your motivations, traits, skills, and resources. Through honest evaluation, you can gain clarity and make an informed decision. Keep in mind that entrepreneurship is dynamic, and readiness can evolve. Seek guidance from experienced entrepreneurs and mentors for valuable insights during this transformative journey.

Entrepreneurship necessitates passion, resilience, adaptability, risk-taking, and purpose. It grants the freedom to pursue passions, makes an impact, and shape destiny. Carefully considering the factors discussed helps determine if entrepreneurship aligns with your aspirations. Take confident steps toward building a successful and fulfilling entrepreneurial career.

SERIES TWO
IDEA GENERATION AND VALIDATION

Ideation encompasses the creative process of generating, developing, and communicating new business ideas. When initiating a new business, we can either adopt an existing concept or cultivate our distinct idea. This also holds for expanding an established enterprise. The true challenge is determining whether an idea has the potential to be a strong foundation for a successful business, even though coming up with ideas may be very straightforward. Once you have what you consider a "great idea," the next hurdle is to validate or test its viability as a successful venture.

At times, finding a viable idea can be the most challenging aspect. It may appear as if all the promising ideas have been explored, leaving you with the resources and ambition to initiate or expand a business but needing a remarkable concept. The ideation process varies in duration, ranging from a single day to several years, and similar to the creative process, rushing tends to yield unproductive results. Apart from the usual obstacles of limited resources (financial and human), the absence of a "good idea" often deters individuals from pursuing their dream of becoming entrepreneurs.

The foundation of building a new business lies in the idea itself. This involves developing and refining your business concept, which requires prototyping and iterating. Your idea will evolve into something entirely new in the early stages. Business ideas can generally be categorized into three main groups, and exploring these categories can stimulate fresh ideas or provide validation for existing ones.

Now - a new invention or business idea

The "New" category represents the most challenging realm for business ideas - entirely novel and groundbreaking. Genuine new ideas, which have never existed before, are exceptionally rare. It's crucial to differentiate between a new idea and an improvement or disruption of an existing or conventional approach. While genuinely unique ideas are hard to find, it's essential to avoid becoming paralyzed by the notion that they are the only source of viable new concepts.

Improvement - the proverbial improved mouse trap

The second category encompasses most small businesses. It involves taking an existing product or service and improving it directly or indirectly. This could include using higher quality materials in manufacturing, enhancing the product or service by offering additional features or services, or finding ways to deliver it more efficiently. By improving existing offerings, businesses can differentiate themselves and provide enhanced value to customers.

Disruption - a novel and innovative method of doing something

The internet and other modern technologies have revolutionized our interconnected world, enabling us to reimagine and disrupt entire industries completely. While they are not the sole means of executing disruptive business ideas, they have significantly accelerated our capacity. These new possibilities for innovation and change have allowed entrepreneurs to restructure sectors and launch groundbreaking businesses.

Maintaining a competitive edge in today's dynamic business landscape necessitates a continuous stream of innovative ideas and solutions. The generation and validation of ideas are crucial for the success of any organization, serving as the bedrock for product development, process enhancement, and overall business expansion. By fostering a culture of creativity and embracing the iterative process of idea generation, companies can position themselves for sustained growth and adaptability.

The Importance Of Having A Solid Business Idea

A strong and well-defined idea is the cornerstone of entrepreneurial triumph in the ever-evolving business landscape. A compelling business idea guides a company's strategy, operations, and overall trajectory. It acts as the driving force that propels a venture forward, attracting crucial stakeholders such as investors, partners, and talented individuals. Confidence is instilled with an enticing business idea, paving the way for securing funding and assembling a capable team to turn aspirations into tangible achievements.

Understanding the Significance of a Solid Business Idea

1. Vision and Clarity

A strong business idea offers entrepreneurs an ideal vision of their aspirations and objectives. It acts as a guiding beacon, illuminating the business's purpose, values, and mission. With a clearly defined idea, entrepreneurs can effectively communicate their vision to stakeholders, employees, and investors, fostering unity and dedication.

2. Market Relevance

A robust business idea resonates with the market, addressing genuine needs and fulfilling unmet demands. Through comprehensive market research, entrepreneurs can identify gaps, pain points, and opportunities, allowing them to customize their products or services to meet customer requirements. By delivering a distinctive value proposition, businesses with relevant ideas can gain a competitive advantage and establish themselves as industry frontrunners.

3. Differentiation and Unique Selling Proposition (USP)

In today's crowded markets, differentiation is essential to thrive. A strong business idea empowers entrepreneurs to set themselves apart by emphasizing a unique selling proposition (USP). This distinctive quality distinguishes the business from competitors, attracting customers and securing a solid market position, ultimately driving long-term growth and profitability.

4. Scalability and Growth Potential

A carefully crafted business idea forms the basis for scalability and future growth. Entrepreneurs must evaluate their idea's scalability prospects, considering operational scalability, market size, and demand. An idea with solid scalability potential can attract the necessary resources, including investors and partners, to support expansion efforts, securing the business's long-term viability and success.

5. Adaptability and Innovation

A strong business idea enables entrepreneurs to navigate evolving market dynamics with adaptability and innovation. By embracing flexibility, businesses can effectively respond to emerging trends, changing customer preferences, and technological advancements. Additionally, a solid idea cultivates an innovative mindset, inspiring entrepreneurs to seek new solutions and seize growth opportunities continuously.

6. Convince Investors and Partners

In the competitive entrepreneurship landscape, a strong business idea holds the power to captivate investors and partners. It enables entrepreneurs to craft a persuasive narrative highlighting a clear value proposition, sustainable market advantage, and growth potential. Investors are drawn to ventures that showcase these qualities, as they signify promising opportunities for resource allocation. Similarly, partners are attracted to ideas that align with their objectives and offer mutually beneficial prospects. A robust business idea establishes trust and generates interest among potential investors and partners, laying a solid foundation for collaboration and growth.

7. Attract the Right Team Members and Advisors

Assembling the right team is vital for business success, and a strong business idea acts as a magnetic force, attracting talented individuals who align with the venture's vision and goals. Exceptional team members are motivated by purpose and drawn to projects offering an exciting and viable future. Advisors also gravitate towards ventures with solid business ideas, recognizing their potential for success and wanting to contribute their expertise. With a robust business idea, entrepreneurs can gather a passionate team of individuals dedicated to achieving shared objectives.

A solid business idea is the cornerstone of successful ventures. It offers entrepreneurs a clear vision, market relevance, differentiation, scalability, and adaptability. Through iterative processes, adaptation, and a well-crafted business plan, entrepreneurs can navigate the dynamic business landscape and turn their ideas into thriving enterprises. Remembering that a solid business idea serves as the starting point and fuels the drive toward entrepreneurial success is essential.

How To Generate Business Ideas

Contrary to popular opinion, anyone can develop a compelling business idea. Creating business ideas is a relatively easy task. The true challenge, though, is finding a concept that appeals to your personality, meets your needs, and has the potential to be successful.

At this stage, numerous aspiring entrepreneurs often encounter a dilemma. They possess a burning desire to start their own business but are still determining the specific type of business to pursue. The weighty question, "What kind of business should I start?" looms over them as they recognize that the nature of their chosen venture can profoundly impact their ultimate success.

Having a framework or set of guidelines to channel your thinking toward business ideas that align with your unique situation is a significant stride toward achieving success in entrepreneurship. Let's explore some valuable tips to assist you in generating exceptional business ideas.

❖ **Activate your mind and engage in active thinking**

Fear not if you are bogged down by the daily grind or unable to let your creativity run free because of mental limitations. This series provides helpful advice and direction to fire your creative process and critical thinking skills.

The brain is divided into two leading hemispheres: the right and the left. Each hemisphere has distinct functions and operates in unique ways. Using visual aspects like shapes, colors, and images to assess and process information, the right hemisphere is in charge of creativity and artistic ability. It plays a crucial role in fostering imagination and controlling creative thinking processes.

The brain's left hemisphere is the logical part, responsible for mathematical calculations, identifying causes and effects, using words for description and definition, and controlling speech, grammar, and word order. It excels in analytical thinking and language processing.

It's crucial to balance both sides of the brain to succeed in business. Cultivating your imaginative and creative abilities enables you to generate innovative business ideas and find creative solutions to entrepreneurial challenges. Simultaneously, leveraging your logical faculties allows you to analyze and define business opportunities, calculate risks, and make informed decisions to address business issues. Striking a harmonious balance between creativity and logic is key to thriving entrepreneurship.

The brain is akin to a muscle that requires regular exercise to stay in shape. Just as you cannot prepare for a marathon by remaining sedentary on the couch, you cannot foster creative thinking without actively engaging your mind. Common obstacles to creativity include ingrained habits, limiting attitudes, rigid routines, self-doubt, and excessive reliance on external guidance. Overcoming these barriers involves:

- Cultivating an open mind.
- Being receptive to new experiences.
- Embracing fresh challenges.
- Permitting yourself to think creatively.

Dedicate time to thought and stimulate your brain to unlock its creative potential.

The change is a powerful catalyst for stimulating the brain and uncovering fresh ideas. By altering your surroundings, you can free your mind from the constraints of daily concerns and gain clarity to foster creative thinking. Whether visiting a garden, a beach, or any place that appeals to you, exercising your brain in a different environment can be immensely beneficial.

Interacting with different individuals can also be instrumental in your creative process. By engaging with new people and actively listening to their challenges and frustrations, you can gain valuable insights into their needs and aspirations – a foundation for success in any business. Additionally, exploring new locations can lead to discovering previously unseen or unheard-of innovative ideas. Perhaps during a trip to another city, you come across a unique store concept that you believe would thrive in your city. Embracing these changes in people and places can spark fresh ideas and open up new possibilities.

In the long run, finding fresh ideas can be done without traveling to far-off places. Even modest changes to your daily routine can make a significant difference.

❖ **Get a notebook**

Having learned how to stimulate your brain and initiate the creative thinking process, tracking and documenting your ideas for further study and examination is essential.

Every business begins with a small idea that can originate from simple observations, frustrating situations, or even moments of reflection. The critical difference lies in those who take the time to nurture and enhance these ideas, transforming them into successful ventures. Because inspiration can strike at any time, keeping a notebook nearby is critical to jot down these ideas as they occur.

❖ **Follow your passion**

Selecting a business that ignites your passion and excitement is crucial when embarking on your entrepreneurial journey. Enjoying what you do is paramount, as you'll devote most of your time to your venture for years. The likelihood of success diminishes if you lack enthusiasm for your chosen business. This disparity is not always a lack of expertise but rather the risk of losing interest when faced with inevitable hurdles.

Launching and growing a thriving business is a substantial undertaking, demanding significant effort and presenting numerous challenges. You'll encounter unfamiliar situations and encounter various obstacles along the way. That's why it's crucial to pursue something you genuinely adore. When faced with adversity, your passion becomes the driving force that propels you forward and enables you to surmount hurdles. Without a genuine love for your endeavor, you may be inclined to seek an early exit when confronted with difficulties.

Moreover, when you engage in something you love and comprehend its underlying motivations, you can better fulfill customer needs. Understanding customer needs and the reasons behind purchasing decisions is fundamental to comprehending your business and guaranteeing its triumph.

Considering this, it is crucial to assess the demand and determine if there is a willingness among people to pay for the product or service when transforming an old hobby into a new business. Conducting thorough calculations and market research is crucial to ensure sufficient interest from potential customers. Otherwise, pursuing something that may not attract a significant audience is risky.

❖ Stay observant

New business prospects arise from evolving circumstances constantly. Cultivate the habit of staying informed about your surroundings by regularly reading the newspaper and being aware of current events. Pay attention to any concerns or issues people raise, such as inadequate healthcare services or a scarcity of schools in your local community. These observations can unveil potential opportunities to address and create a successful business.

Engage in meaningful conversations with neighbors and acquaintances to uncover their frustrations and aspirations. What improvements do they desire for the neighborhood? Does your neighbor express discontent with the long commute to the nearest dry cleaner? Are others dissatisfied with the lack of nearby grocery options? Perhaps your coworkers long for convenient restaurants near your workplace. By understanding these needs, you can identify potential business opportunities that cater to local demands.

Stay vigilant to seize emerging opportunities by remaining attentive to new developments and changes in your surroundings. Success sometimes requires an original or unique business idea; often, tried-and-tested concepts can lead to prosperity. Take a closer look at your local area, identify the gaps or unmet needs, and consider filling them with your venture. Observing and responding to what is missing could uncover your next business endeavor.

❖ Focus on your strengths

Assess your experiences and career to identify your areas of expertise. This is often an ideal starting point if you have a long-standing project management background and possess comprehensive industry knowledge.

Fear of establishing a business typically arises from focusing on one's flaws and believing that failure is certain due to deficiencies. Remember that no one is flawless; running a successful business does not necessitate superhuman powers.

Redirect your attention from your weaknesses to your strengths. Identify what you excel at and consider how you can outperform others. Explore existing approaches and envision innovative alternatives. Starting a business may require a fresh idea or even a slight modification to an established one. If your industry needs to catch up in its business practices, you might discover an opportunity to introduce automation or computerization to streamline processes and manage records more efficiently.

Direct your attention to your areas of extensive knowledge and expertise. These areas can extend beyond your professional experience. For instance, if you excel at assisting friends with their finances, consider leveraging this skill by starting a business offering individuals personal financial planning services.

❖ Try new things

As previously stated, change is a significant catalyst for stimulating the brain. Even if opening a coffee shop is different from your intention, take the opportunity to observe and evaluate the operations of a coffee shop. Explore potential improvements and consider how these insights can be applied to enhance your business ideas within your industry.

Surprisingly, attending a business meeting in a different location can unexpectedly spark your next business idea. The more diverse your experiences are, the broader your range of possibilities, enabling you to generate fresh ideas and adopt innovative thinking.

❖ Examine your financial strength

Consider your financial constraints when generating business ideas. Choosing ventures that align with your budget is crucial, as everyone has limited funds. Ensure that the business idea you pursue is feasible within your financial means.

If you have limited funds, consider capital-efficient business ideas that allow for gradual growth. Additionally, explore various financing options such as banks, venture capital firms, family, friends, and local small business associations. Determine the amount of financing you can secure in advance and focus on business opportunities that fall within those financial limits.

While seeking external financial assistance for your business offers certain advantages, it often entails sharing ownership or taking on debt. It's crucial to weigh these options carefully and determine whether you are comfortable with the associated risks. Consider whether you prefer to maintain complete control and bear financial responsibility independently.

❖ Know your want

In addition to your business objectives, reflect on the underlying reasons driving your decision to start a business. What are your aspirations? What are your life goals? Is it to achieve a better work-life balance and spend more time with family? Is it to increase your financial earnings? Is it to gain recognition and respect within your professional community?

Align your business idea with your goals to ensure they harmoniously support and enable your aspirations. If you aim to prioritize family time and pursue other interests, there might be better options than starting a business that demands 16-hour workdays or frequent travel. Consider a venture that allows for flexibility and balance, granting you the freedom to achieve your desired lifestyle.

Contrary to popular belief, money is often not the primary motivation for starting a business. While financial freedom is undoubtedly a significant benefit, the type and operation of a business are influenced by factors beyond monetary considerations alone. Any business has the potential to generate income; however, other factors play a vital role in shaping the nature and direction of the venture.

❖ Choose a business that suits your personality

Consider your preference for mornings or evenings. Each person has their peak hours of productivity. Successful bakers and newspaper owners are typically early risers. If you're not a morning person, steer clear of businesses that demand early morning work. On the other hand, running a nightclub or a late-night restaurant might be more suitable if you thrive at night. Conversely, if you prefer sleeping early, managing a business that requires late-night commitments may not be the best fit.

Are you more inclined towards indoor or outdoor settings? Do you thrive in an office environment, dedicating long hours to work, or do you feel restless and prefer staying on the move? Consider choosing a business that can be operated from a fixed location if you value the peace of an office. If you prefer being constantly on the go, choose a career that demands you to visit diverse locations and connect with new people.

Individuals differ in their preferred methods for approaching tasks. While some people love mentally demanding hobbies, others find contentment in practical labor and craftsmanship.

Do you consider yourself shy or outgoing? If you lean towards shyness, there may be more suitable paths than pursuing a career as a public speaker. An internet-based business, however, can deprive you of that enjoyment if you have an outgoing personality and love frequently socializing with new people. Reflect on your unique qualities and characteristics to select a business idea that aligns with your personality.

❖ **Discover the experiences of individuals who have launched their businesses.**

Studying accomplished individuals and gaining insights into their paths to success is crucial to succeed as an entrepreneur. By reading autobiographies of prominent and successful business figures, you can learn valuable lessons about their strategies, actions, and the key factors behind their success.

Most of these entrepreneurs began with nothing, experiencing multiple business failures and enduring discouragement from those who doubted their potential for success. However, they persevered, repeatedly picking themselves up and trying again until they ultimately achieved their goals. It's not the act of failing that defines one's character, but rather the determination to rise after each setback.

Analyze their personalities and identify common traits among successful individuals. Explore how they realized their visions and conquered obstacles. Seek parallels between their narratives and your current circumstances. This exploration will serve as a powerful source of inspiration and motivation. If others in similar situations have achieved success, you have the potential to surpass their accomplishments.

How To Validate Your Business Idea

Having conceived a brilliant business idea, the subsequent crucial stage is to convert it into a flourishing venture. However, before investing your valuable time, energy, and resources, it is imperative to validate your business idea. Validation involves verifying if your idea possesses the potential to thrive in the market. This process aids in avoiding costly errors and enhances your prospects of establishing a successful business. The following steps are pivotal in validating your business idea and positioning yourself for triumph.

Step 1: Define Your Target Audience

The first stage in validating your business idea is determining your target market. Who are your products or services potential customers? Understanding your target market's needs, desires, and problems is crucial for ensuring a market for your products.

Start by conducting market research. Identify your potential customers and gather information about their demographics, behaviors, and purchasing patterns. Look for trends, insights, and gaps in the market that your idea can address. You can modify your service to match your target audience's particular needs with this study's aid.

Step 2: Conduct a Competitor Analysis

Competitors are already in the market, no matter how unique your business idea may seem. Competitor analysis is vital to understand the landscape you're entering and identifying how your idea can stand out.

Research your competitors thoroughly. Identify their strengths, weaknesses, and unique selling propositions. Determine what sets your idea apart and how it can provide additional value to customers. Differentiation is critical to carving out a niche for your business idea and attracting customers in a crowded market.

Step 3: Test Your Minimum Viable Product (MVP)

Making an MVP is essential for proving that your business idea is viable. You can evaluate the viability of your good or service and gather feedback from potential customers by creating a minimal viable product (MVP).

Create a prototype or a basic version of your product that showcases its core features and functionalities. Share your MVP with your target audience and gather their feedback. Pay attention to their reactions, suggestions, and pain points they identify. This feedback will provide valuable insights on improving and refining your offering.

Step 4: Seek Feedback from Potential Customers

The opinions of prospective clients help validate your business idea. Interact with your target audience by conducting interviews, focus groups, or surveys. Asking open-ended questions will help you understand your clients' needs, preferences, and willingness to pay for your product or service.

Listen carefully to their responses and use their feedback to iterate and enhance your business idea. This feedback loop ensures you align your offering with the market's demands and expectations.

Step 5: Evaluate Revenue Generation Potential

Assessing the possibility of money creation is essential to validate your business idea. Can you charge for your products or services? How much are they willing to spend?

Consider conducting pricing experiments or market tests to gauge customers' price sensitivity. Offer discounts, limited-time offers, or different pricing tiers to understand their willingness to pay and the value they perceive in your offering. This data will help you determine the pricing strategy that maximizes your revenue while remaining attractive to customers.

Step 6: Build a Proof of Concept

A proof of concept provides tangible evidence that your business idea is viable and can deliver value to customers. It demonstrates the feasibility of your idea and builds credibility with potential investors, partners, and stakeholders.

Develop a more refined version of your product or service that showcases its capabilities and potential impact. This can include a functional prototype, a pilot project, or a case study. The proof of concept is a persuasive tool to garner support and investment for your business idea.

Step 7: Iterate and Refine

Validation is an ongoing process, and it's essential to iterate and refine your business idea based on the feedback and insights you receive. Use the information gathered from testing your MVP, seeking customer feedback, and evaluating revenue potential to make necessary adjustments and improvements.

Be open to adapting your idea to meet the needs of your target audience better and differentiate yourself from competitors. Embrace feedback as an opportunity for growth and innovation. You increase its chances of success in the market by continuously iterating and refining your business idea.

Step 8: Assess Scalability and Long-Term Viability

While your business idea may show promise initially, assessing its scalability and long-term viability is crucial. Consider the potential challenges and opportunities that may arise as your business grows.

Evaluate factors such as scalability of operations, customer acquisition and retention strategies, and potential expansion into new markets. Determine whether your idea has the potential for long-term, profitable growth. You may make wise judgments and create a strong company plan for the future with the aid of this assessment.

Step 9: Test the Market

Before fully launching your business, consider conducting a market test to validate your idea further. This can involve running a small-scale pilot or beta program to gauge customer interest, collect additional feedback, and refine your offering based on real-world experiences.

Market testing allows you to validate assumptions, identify any remaining issues or challenges, and fine-tune your business model. Use the insights gained during this phase to make necessary adjustments before scaling up your operations.

Step 10: Seek Guidance and Expert Advice

Validating your business idea can be complex, and seeking guidance and expert advice can provide invaluable support. Connect with mentors, industry experts, or experienced entrepreneurs who can provide insights and help you navigate the challenges of validating your idea.

Join entrepreneurial communities, attend networking events, and leverage online resources to tap into a wealth of knowledge and expertise. Engaging with individuals in your profession can lead to new insights, spur creativity, and help you steer clear of frequent traps.

Building a successful business requires you first to validate your idea. You can make sure that your idea has a solid basis and a higher chance of success by following these steps.

Remember, validation is an iterative process. Embrace feedback, be adaptable, and continuously refine your business idea based on market insights. With a validated and well-refined concept, you can confidently pursue your entrepreneurial dreams and turn them into a reality.

How To Conduct Market Research

Market research is a fundamental pillar for achieving success in any business venture. It offers a priceless understanding of customer preferences, market trends, and competition, empowering businesses to make well-informed decisions and gain a competitive advantage. Comprehensive market research is vital to introduce a new product, explore new markets, or improve your current offerings.

A crucial task for marketing specialists is conducting market research, which involves gathering data about existing and potential customers. This valuable information enables you to enhance your branding efforts, improve the public perception of your business, and ultimately boost brand recognition and sales.

You are better equipped to create a winning marketing plan for your company when you thoroughly understand your specialized market and its target audience. That is why marketing roles hold such significance for the prosperity of any company, regardless of the product, service, or demographics involved.

A marketing specialist or researcher follows standard steps when conducting a market survey. These steps are pursued for specific reasons. Let's explore the following steps and their purpose:

Step 1: Define Your Research Objectives

Before delving into market research, defining your research objectives is crucial. What specific questions or challenges do you aim to address? Focus on your research efforts and ensure you obtain the right information to support your business decisions by being clear about your decisions.

Consider the aspects you want to explore, such as customer demographics, buying behaviors, market size, or competitor analysis. You can design a research plan that effectively meets your needs by establishing clear objectives.

Step 2: Identify Your Target Audience

Identifying your target audience is a fundamental step in market research. To create efficient marketing strategies and customize your services to your target market's needs, it is crucial to comprehend your potential clients and what drives them. Start by developing buyer personas or consumer profiles. These fictitious portrayals of your ideal clients should include important psychographics, preferences, and pain areas.

By visualizing your target audience, you can tailor your research to gather insights that directly resonate with their needs.

Step 3: Select the Right Research Methodology

Market research can be conducted using various methodologies, each with strengths and limitations. Depending on your research objectives, budget, and timeline, you can choose from primary, secondary, or a combination.

Primary research entails gathering information from your target audience using surveys, interviews, focus groups, or observation. Secondary research involves analyzing data and sources such as industry reports, market studies, and competitor analysis. It offers a cost-effective way to gather information quickly, but it may need more specificity of primary research.

Select the research methodology that aligns with your objectives and resources, and consider combining primary and secondary research for a comprehensive understanding of the market.

Step 4: Design Data Collection Instruments

Once you have determined the research methodology, it's time to design the data collection instruments. Primary research includes creating surveys, interview guides, or discussion frameworks. Remember the research objectives and ensure the questions are clear, unbiased, and relevant to gather meaningful insights.

When crafting surveys or interview questions, employing a combination of closed-ended and open-ended questions is advisable. Closed-ended questions offer predefined response options, enabling participants to choose from specific answers. On the other hand, open-ended questions encourage participants to express their thoughts and opinions freely, using their own words.

This blend of question types allows for a comprehensive analysis of the gathered data, encompassing quantitative insights from closed-ended questions and qualitative perspectives from open-ended responses. By incorporating both questions, you can capture a broader range of information and better understand your target audience's perceptions and experiences.

Step 5: Collect and Analyze Data

With your data collection instruments ready, it's time to collect data from your target audience. Implement your surveys, conduct interviews, or organize focus groups, ensuring you reach a representative sample of your target market.

As data collection progresses, keep track of the responses and ensure data integrity. Once data is collected, it's time to analyze the gathered information. Use statistical tools, data visualization techniques, and qualitative analysis to uncover patterns, trends, and insights within the data.

Step 6: Interpret and Draw Conclusions

Interpretation of the data is a crucial step in market research. Analyze the findings in light of your research objectives and identify key patterns, trends, and emerging insights. Look for market opportunities, challenges, and gaps that can guide your business decisions.

Consider both quantitative and qualitative data to get a comprehensive understanding of the market landscape. Look for correlations, outliers, and emerging themes that can shape your conclusions.

While analyzing the data, it is crucial to be attentive to the findings' nuances and context. Considering the broader market trends, consumer behaviors, and industry dynamics that impact the results is essential. Adopting this holistic approach ensures that your conclusions are firmly rooted in a comprehensive market understanding. Think about the outside influences that can affect your results and interpret them in the context of the overall industry landscape. This perspective will enable you to draw more accurate and insightful conclusions, leading to well-informed decision-making and strategic planning for your business.

Step 7: Validate Findings through Peer Review or Testing

To enhance the reliability of your market research findings, consider seeking validation through peer review or testing.

Share your results with industry experts, colleagues, or trusted advisors and seek their feedback and insights. Their perspectives provide additional validation and offer new views that may uncover new opportunities or challenges.

In addition, consider conducting small-scale tests or pilot programs to validate your findings in real-world scenarios. Launching a limited edition of your product or service to a select group of customers and asking for feedback may be necessary to confirm your assumptions and improve your offering.

Step 8: Apply the Insights to Your Business Strategy

Market research is only valuable when its insights are translated into actionable strategies. Take the findings from your research and apply them to your business strategy. To effectively meet your customers' needs, you must distinguish yourself from competitors and develop marketing strategies that deeply resonate with your target audience.

Consider the implications of your research findings on pricing, distribution channels, branding, and customer experience. To increase your chances of financial success, align your business strategy with the knowledge you have obtained.

Step 9: Continuously Monitor the Market

Market research is not a one-time activity but an ongoing process. As market dynamics change, consumer preferences evolve, and new competitors enter the scene, staying informed and monitoring the market continuously is crucial.

Set up mechanisms to track market trends, customer feedback, and competitor activities. Stay engaged with your target audience through surveys, social media listening, and customer feedback channels. This ongoing monitoring will help you stay ahead of the curve, identify emerging opportunities or threats, and adapt your strategies accordingly.

Step 10: Revisit and Update Your Research

Market research should be revisited and updated periodically to ensure its relevance. New research questions may arise as your business grows and evolves, and existing assumptions may need reevaluation.

Regularly reassess your research objectives and consider conducting new studies or gathering fresh data to address any gaps or changes in the market. By staying proactive and keeping your research up to date, you can make well-informed decisions and maintain a competitive edge.

Conducting market research is a fundamental aspect of building a successful business. It provides essential insights into your target audience, industry landscape, and competitive positioning. Market research empowers you to identify opportunities, mitigate risks, and differentiate yourself in a competitive marketplace. Embrace the power of research and let it guide your path to success as you navigate the exciting business world.

SERIES THREE
BUSINESS PLANNING AND STRATEGY

Imagine going to a foreign destination without a tourist guide or map. Suddenly realizing that you're lost and clueless would be terrifying. Thankfully, people plan their trips to avoid such experiences. Similarly, running a business without a proper plan is akin to traveling without a map. You wouldn't want to invest valuable time into building a business only to realize abruptly that you're unsure of your whereabouts or next steps.

Entrepreneurs often get caught up in the daily responsibilities of building their businesses, neglecting the importance of proper planning. The business owner often needs to allocate more time for future planning.

Within the dynamic realm of business, planning, and strategy is the guiding compass for entrepreneurs on their path to success. A meticulously crafted business plan and strategic mindset are vital for establishing a prosperous and enduring enterprise. They furnish a roadmap, a framework, and a vision that propel businesses towards progress, empowering them to surmount obstacles, capitalize on opportunities, and accomplish their objectives.

Business planning entails envisioning the future of your venture and delineating the required steps to manifest that vision. It is a fluid and cyclical process that involves setting objectives, evaluating the market, understanding customers, identifying resources, and devising a thorough roadmap. A robust business plan serves as a roadmap for success and a compelling instrument when seeking investments or partnerships.

Yet, more than a well-constructed business plan is needed. The strategy complements planning by offering the necessary tactics and actions to realize desired outcomes. Strategic thinking encompasses scrutinizing the competitive landscape, discerning strengths and weaknesses, identifying opportunities, and crafting a distinctive value proposition. It entails making informed decisions and undertaking calculated risks to attain a competitive edge in the market.

Whether initiating a startup, scaling an established business, or seeking innovation within your industry, proficient business planning and strategy are indispensable. They empower you to outline a distinct path, allocate resources effectively, and make well-informed decisions that propel your business toward enduring success.

Sound business planning and strategy yield extensive advantages. They facilitate the identification of your target market, comprehend customer needs, and effectively position your products or services. A meticulously crafted plan empowers you to anticipate challenges, mitigate risks, and capitalize on growth prospects. It also allows efficient resource allocation, streamlined financial management, and the establishment of tangible milestones to gauge your progress.

No matter how much or little entrepreneurial experience you have, you must invest time and energy into developing a sound business strategy and a strategic mindset. Demonstrating such dedication to the continuous success of your business speaks volumes about your passion, unwavering commitment, and forward-thinking mindset.

In this series, we will explore the essential components of a well-rounded business plan, delve into the intricacies of strategic thinking, and provide practical insights and tools to help you develop and implement a winning strategy.

Creating A Business Plan That Addresses Challenges

In the realm of entrepreneurship, challenges are unavoidable. From intense competition to shifting market dynamics, entrepreneurs encounter numerous obstacles in their pursuit of success. Nevertheless, engaging in thoughtful planning and adopting a proactive mindset can transform these challenges into avenues for growth and innovation. A meticulously designed business plan that directly tackles these challenges is vital for entrepreneurs to navigate the dynamic business landscape and cultivate a flourishing venture.

A business plan acts as a roadmap, offering your business a precise direction and strategic structure. It articulates your vision, mission, goals, and the strategies necessary to accomplish them. However, in addition to the customary components of a business plan, effectively addressing challenges demands a comprehensive comprehension of the potential obstacles you may face and the corresponding strategies to overcome them.

The initial step in crafting a business plan that effectively tackles challenges is identifying and comprehending the industry-specific, target market, and competitive landscape obstacles. Conducting thorough market research empowers you to gain insights into customer requirements, competitor tactics, and emerging trends. This knowledge serves as the bedrock for formulating strategies that set you apart in the market and surmount obstacles.

A comprehensive business plan should address the following challenges:

1. Funding

One of the common challenges faced by entrepreneurs is securing funding. Financial constraints can hinder growth and sustainability, Whether seeking investment from venture capitalists or obtaining a small business loan. Addressing this challenge in your business plan involves:

- Clearly articulating your financial needs
- Outlining a comprehensive budget

- Developing a robust financial strategy

Demonstrating a solid understanding of your revenue streams, cost structure, and projected financial performance will increase your chances of securing funding.

2. Technology

Another significant challenge for businesses is adapting to a rapidly evolving technological landscape. Technological advancements can disrupt industries and render traditional business models obsolete. To address this challenge, your business plan should incorporate strategies to embrace innovation and leverage technology to your advantage. This may entail making research and development investments, encouraging innovation within your company, and keeping abreast of market developments and new technological trends.

3. Competition

Market competition is another critical challenge that entrepreneurs must tackle. Understanding your competitive landscape and developing strategies to differentiate your business is essential. Your business plan should outline your unique value proposition, positioning in the market, and how you will outperform your competitors. This may involve leveraging your strengths, exploring niche markets, or offering innovative products or services that meet unmet customer needs.

4. Operation

Operational challenges, such as supply chain management, production efficiency, and scaling operations, can pose significant hurdles. Addressing these challenges requires a detailed operational plan within your business plan. This plan should outline how you will optimize your processes, ensure quality control, and manage growth effectively. Identifying potential bottlenecks and developing contingency plans will enhance your operational resilience and enable you to navigate challenges smoothly.

5. Team-building

Another key challenge is building a solid team. Any business's success relies heavily on its employees' skills, expertise, and commitment. In your business plan, address how you will attract and retain top talent. Clearly define your organizational structure, outline your recruitment and retention strategies, and emphasize your company culture and values. Demonstrating a compelling vision and offering competitive compensation and growth opportunities will help you build a dedicated, high-performing team.

6. Risk management

Incorporating risk management into your business plan is vital for effectively addressing challenges. When you proactively identify potential risks and devise effective strategies to mitigate them, you showcase your foresight and preparedness, paving the way for a more resilient and secure journey towards your goals. It is crucial to analyze both internal and external risks within your business plan. These risks include economic fluctuations, legal and regulatory changes, and operational vulnerabilities. You can develop appropriate risk mitigation strategies and contingency plans by identifying and understanding these risks. Additionally, your business plan should incorporate a comprehensive approach to business continuity, ensuring that your operations can continue uninterrupted despite potential challenges.

7. Adaptability and flexibility

It is essential to foster a mindset of agility and adaptability within your business plan. Recognize that the business landscape constantly evolves, and new challenges may emerge. Incorporate flexibility into your business plan, allowing adjustments and iterations as needed. This can include conducting regular performance evaluations, monitoring key performance indicators, and revisiting your strategies and tactics to ensure they align with your goals.

8. Collaboration

Building solid relationships and partnerships can help you address challenges effectively. Collaborating with suppliers, strategic alliances, and industry networks can provide valuable support and resources. In your business plan, outline your approach to fostering partnerships and building a solid network to help you collectively navigate challenges.

9. Communication

Communication is also a critical factor in addressing challenges. Your business plan should emphasize effective internal and external communication strategies. Internally, establish clear communication channels to ensure everyone in your organization is informed, aligned, and empowered to address challenges proactively. Externally, consider how you will communicate with stakeholders, customers, and partners, keeping them informed and engaged throughout your journey.

Creating a business plan that addresses challenges requires a proactive and strategic approach. By conducting thorough market research, understanding your industry landscape, and identifying potential obstacles, you can develop strategies to overcome them.

Ultimately, a well-crafted business plan that addresses challenges demonstrates your preparedness and resilience and increases your chances of long-term success. As a guiding document, your business plan plays a crucial role in navigating the unpredictable path of entrepreneurship. By anticipating and proactively addressing challenges, you not only steer your business through obstacles but also create an environment conducive to growth, innovation, and long-term success.

It is important to devote time to assess potential challenges that your business may face, develop effective strategies to overcome them, and integrate these strategies into your comprehensive business plan. With careful planning, resilience, and a proactive mindset, you can turn challenges into stepping stones toward achieving your entrepreneurial dreams. Embrace the opportunities that challenge present, and let your business plan be the roadmap that leads you to success. Regularly review and revise your plan as circumstances change and new challenges arise.

Developing A Long-Term Business Strategy

Maintaining growth can prove challenging for companies, even during favorable economic conditions. The contemporary business landscape is characterized by constant change:

- The information highway remains vibrant.
- Technology advances rapidly.
- Distribution channels unexpectedly shift.
- New competitors emerge daily.

Consequently, a long-term strategy is indispensable for attaining sustainable growth and retaining a competitive edge.

An effectively crafted business strategy serves as a roadmap, directing decision-making, resource allocation, and the overall trajectory of your organization. It establishes the groundwork for success by harmonizing your vision, goals, and actions while adapting to evolving market dynamics and emerging opportunities.

Developing a comprehensive long-term business strategy necessitates a holistic and forward-thinking approach. It entails gaining profound insights into your business, industry, customers, and competitive environment. By prioritizing long-term objectives over immediate gains, you can establish the foundation for sustainable growth and cultivate a competitive edge.

Understand your position

To begin crafting a long-term business strategy, assessing your current position and identifying your strengths, weaknesses, opportunities, and threats is essential. You can learn more about your internal resources and outside elements that may have an impact on your success by conducting this analysis, often known as a SWOT analysis.

Identifying your strengths helps you leverage your unique advantages and core competencies. These include a strong brand reputation, a talented team, proprietary technology, and a robust distribution network. By understanding and capitalizing on your strengths, you can differentiate yourself in the market and build a sustainable competitive advantage.

Simultaneously, it is crucial to identify and address your weaknesses. These can be areas where your organization may need more resources, outdated technology, or operational inefficiencies. Acknowledging and addressing these weaknesses, you can develop strategies to overcome them and enhance your overall performance.

While assessing your internal factors, evaluating external opportunities and threats is equally important. Opportunities can arise from market trends, emerging technologies, or changes in customer behavior. Identifying and seizing these opportunities can propel your business forward and open new avenues for growth. On the other hand, threats can come from factors such as increased competition, regulatory changes, or economic fluctuations. Understanding these threats enables you to develop strategies to mitigate risks and navigate challenges effectively.

Define your goals and objectives.

Once you have conducted a comprehensive analysis, it is time to define your long-term goals and objectives. These objectives should meet the SMART criteria of being specific, measurable, achievable, relevant, and time-bound. They have to be consistent with the objectives of your company and show what you hope to accomplish over the long term.

When setting your long-term goals, it is essential to consider financial and non-financial aspects. Financial goals may include revenue targets, profit margins, or return on investment. Non-financial goals can encompass market share, customer satisfaction, brand recognition, or sustainability initiatives. Striking a balance between these goals ensures a well-rounded and holistic approach to long-term success.

Develop strategies

With your goals in place, it is time to develop strategies to achieve them. These strategies outline the broad approach you will take to accomplish your objectives. They encompass various aspects of your business, including market positioning, product or service development, customer acquisition and retention, operational efficiency, and innovation.

1. Market positioning strategy

Market positioning is a critical component of your long-term strategy. It involves identifying your target market segments and developing a unique value proposition that differentiates you from competitors. By understanding your customer's needs and preferences, you can effectively tailor your offerings to meet their demands.

2. Product or service development strategies

These strategies focus on continuously improving and innovating your offerings to stay ahead of the market. To promote innovation and raise consumer happiness, this may entail spending money on research and development, keeping an eye on market trends, and getting customer input.

3. Customer acquisition and retention strategies

For long-term success, these are crucial. You can bring in new clients while fostering enduring relationships with current ones by comprehending your target demographic and putting into practice efficient marketing and sales methods. Customer retention programs, loyalty initiatives, and exceptional customer service can help foster long-term loyalty and maximize customer lifetime value.

4. Operational efficiency strategies

Operational efficiency strategies aim to streamline processes, reduce costs, and enhance productivity within your organization. This can involve implementing technology solutions, optimizing supply chain management, and continually assessing and improving operational workflows. By maximizing efficiency, you can allocate resources effectively and drive profitability.

5. Innovation strategies

These are crucial for long-term success in today's rapidly evolving business landscape. They involve fostering a culture of creativity and continuous improvement within your organization. Encouraging employees to generate and explore new ideas, investing in research and development, and staying abreast of industry trends can help you stay innovative and adapt to changing customer needs.

Turning your strategies into reality

Implementation and execution are key to turning your long-term strategy into a reality. This requires effective project management, clear communication, and the allocation of resources to support strategic initiatives. Establishing key performance indicators (KPIs) and regular monitoring and evaluation processes will enable you to track progress, make necessary adjustments, and ensure alignment with your long-term goals.

Flexibility and adaptability are essential when developing a long-term business strategy. The business landscape constantly evolves, and unforeseen challenges and opportunities may arise. Your strategy should have built-in mechanisms for reassessment and adaptation to ensure its relevance and effectiveness over time. Regularly reviewing and updating your strategy based on market trends, customer feedback, and internal analysis will help you stay agile and responsive to change.

Furthermore, fostering a culture of collaboration and engagement within your organization is crucial. Involving key stakeholders, such as employees, managers, and even customers, in the strategy development process can generate valuable insights and create a sense of ownership. Engaged employees who understand and believe in the long-term strategy are more likely to contribute to its success actively.

Lastly, monitoring and benchmarking against industry trends, competitors, and best practices can provide valuable insights and help you stay ahead of the curve. Keeping a pulse on market dynamics, customer preferences, emerging technologies, and regulatory changes will allow you to adapt your strategy proactively and identify new growth opportunities.

Sustainable growth and profitability need the creation of long-term business strategies. It necessitates in-depth knowledge about your company, market, target audience, and competitors. Implementation, flexibility, and engagement are crucial in turning your strategy into actionable initiatives. Regular monitoring, evaluation, and adaptation will ensure its relevance in a rapidly changing business environment. Embrace the challenge of crafting a long-term strategy and let it propel your organization toward a future of growth and prosperity.

How To Refine And Iterate Your Business Plan

For your entrepreneurial journey, a business plan acts as a road map, guiding your strategies and activities. A static business strategy, however, can quickly become out of date and less effective in the face of shifting market conditions and developing opportunities. To maintain competitiveness and adaptability, continuously refining and iterating your business plan is vital.

Refining your business plan necessitates reassessing and enhancing various facets to align with your present goals, market conditions, and operational realities. Embracing a mindset of ongoing improvement empowers you to pinpoint areas for refinement and implement necessary adjustments, optimizing your likelihood of success.

The following are the areas of concentration when refining your business plan:

- Market analysis

Market analysis is the first key area to focus on when refining your business plan. Markets are ever-changing, influenced by technological advancements, shifting consumer behaviors, and economic trends. Regularly reviewing and updating your market analysis lets you stay informed about the latest trends, identify new opportunities, and assess potential threats. This ensures that your business remains relevant and adaptable to market fluctuations.

- Value proposition

Your value proposition defines the unique value you offer to your target customers. As market dynamics change, it is important to reassess your value proposition to ensure it continues to resonate with your customers and differentiates you from competitors. Conducting customer research, gathering feedback, and monitoring industry trends can provide valuable insights for refining and enhancing your value proposition.

- Financial evaluation and optimization

Refining your business plan involves evaluating and optimizing your financial projections. Review your revenue forecasts, expense projections, and cash flow statements to ensure they accurately reflect your current operational realities. Analyze your financial data, identify areas of improvement, and make adjustments accordingly. This will help you make informed decisions, allocate resources effectively, and maintain financial stability and growth.

In addition to refining existing components, iterating your business plan involves introducing new strategies and tactics based on feedback, market insights, and lessons learned. It requires embracing change and experimenting with new approaches to optimize your business operations.

To iterate effectively, leverage feedback from stakeholders, including customers, employees, investors, and mentors. Their perspectives can provide valuable insights and help identify areas for improvement. Actively seek feedback through surveys, interviews, and open communication channels. Use this feedback to refine your strategies, enhance customer experiences, and drive operational efficiencies.

Another way to iterate your business plan is to stay informed about industry best practices and emerging trends. Continuously educate yourself and your team through industry events, workshops, webinars, and networking opportunities. Explore new technologies, innovative business models, and evolving customer preferences. Take advantage of fresh opportunities and keep one step ahead of the competition by incorporating these insights into your company plan.

Effective iteration demands a culture of ongoing learning and development. Within your organization, promote an attitude of experimentation, creativity, and adaptability. Encourage an atmosphere where employees feel free to share ideas, try out new tactics, and offer feedback. Regularly review and assess the outcomes of your iterations, learning from successes and failures alike, and use this knowledge to refine your business plan further.

Remember that iteration is an ongoing process. As your business evolves and the market landscape changes, you will need to continuously refine and iterate your business plan to ensure its relevance and effectiveness. Regularly schedule dedicated time for plan review and refinement, allowing flexibility and adaptability.

Identifying And Managing Risks

Operating a business entails navigating uncertainty and risk. Identifying and managing these risks is vital to safeguard your business, ensure its longevity, and optimize your prospects for success. By proactively assessing potential risks and implementing robust risk management strategies, you can mitigate adverse consequences and capitalize on opportunities. Let's delve into the essential steps to identify and manage risks within your business.

❖ Identify potential risks

Identification of potential risks is the first stage in risk management. Risks can stem from diverse sources, encompassing both internal and external factors. External factors may include market conditions, shifts in legislation and regulations, and natural disasters. Internally, risks can arise from aspects such as operational procedures, financial management, and human resources. Conduct a comprehensive risk assessment by examining each area of your business and identifying potential risks specific to your industry and operations.

❖ Assess risks impact

Once risks are identified, assessing their potential impact and likelihood is crucial. Categorize risks based on severity and probability, allowing you to prioritize and allocate resources effectively. High-impact, high-probability risks should receive immediate attention, while low-impact risks may require less urgent action. You will focus on the most important areas by using this assessment to direct your risk management activities.

❖ Develop a plan

Develop a risk management plan tailored to your business's unique needs and circumstances. This plan should outline specific strategies and actions to mitigate identified risks. It may include implementing robust financial controls, diversifying your customer base, investing in cyber security systems, or establishing contingency plans for potential disruptions. The plan should be pragmatic, implementable, subject to regular review, and adaptable to reflect the evolving dynamics of your business environment.

❖ Enhance effective communication

Communication is a crucial aspect of effective risk management. Ensure that all relevant stakeholders, including employees, management, and business partners, know the identified risks and the measures in place to mitigate them. Encourage a culture of risk awareness and accountability, empowering employees to report potential risks and providing channels for open communication. Involving stakeholders in risk management enables you to foster collective risk identification and mitigation responsibility.

❖ Monitor the process

Monitoring and regular review of risks are vital to ensure ongoing effectiveness. The business landscape is dynamic, and new risks may emerge over time. Regularly reassess your risks, evaluate the effectiveness of your risk management strategies, and make necessary adjustments. Stay informed about industry trends, technological advancements, and regulatory changes that may impact your risk landscape. By adopting this proactive approach, you will not only stay ahead of potential threats but also seize emerging opportunities, giving your business a competitive edge.

❖ Evaluate Insurance

This can also play a crucial role in risk management. Evaluate your business's insurance needs and consider obtaining appropriate coverage for potential risks. Business interruption insurance, liability insurance, and cyber security insurance are policies that can provide financial protection and mitigate the impact of unexpected events. Consult with insurance professionals to determine the most suitable coverage for your business.

Regularly review your risk management plan, conduct periodic risk assessments, and foster a culture of continuous improvement. Stay proactive and adaptable in identifying and managing risks, positioning your business for long-term success and resilience.

Identifying and managing risks is an integral part of running a successful business. By conducting thorough risk assessments, developing a comprehensive risk management plan, communicating effectively, and monitoring risks continuously, you can protect your business, minimize potential disruptions, and seize opportunities. Embrace risk management as a strategic priority and confidently navigate the path to success.

SERIES FOUR
FUNDING AND FINANCING

With an exceptional business idea that resonates with your passion, you have invested time in research, competitor analysis, marketing planning, and financial forecasting. However, the biggest challenge of starting a business, regardless of scale, is securing the necessary startup funds to sustain it until profitability. Now, the question arises: Where can you obtain the crucial financing for your venture?

Embarking on the entrepreneurial journey is an exciting pursuit that demands passion, commitment, and a clear vision. Yet, securing sufficient funding is paramount to turning your ideas into a flourishing business. Entrepreneurial funding serves as the lifeblood of your growth, furnishing resources to drive innovation, expand operations, and seize market opportunities.

The entrepreneurial funding landscape presents a myriad of options customized to various stages of business growth and distinct funding needs. From seed funding for budding startups to venture capital for rapidly expanding ventures and from traditional bank loans to crowdfunding platforms, comprehending the attributes and suitability of each option is vital for making informed decisions that align with your business requirements.

To navigate the complex terrain of entrepreneurial funding and financing, it is crucial to meticulously assess your business's unique requirements, growth potential, and risk tolerance. Each funding option entails distinct advantages and trade-offs, and selecting the most suitable choice hinges on variables like your growth stage, industry, scalability, and long-term aspirations.

This series will delve deeper into each funding avenue, providing comprehensive insights into their advantages, challenges, and optimal access approaches. It will encompass strategies for crafting a persuasive pitch, cultivating investor and financier relationships, and maximizing your probability of securing the necessary funding.

After securing initial funding, proficient financial management becomes vital for entrepreneurial triumph. It encompasses budgeting, cash flow forecasting, and vigilant monitoring of critical financial metrics. Maintaining precise and current financial records, expense tracking, and regular financial performance reviews are essential. With a clear comprehension of your financial standing, you can make informed choices, identify areas for enhancement, and foster sustainable growth.

Types Of Funding And Financing Options Available To Entrepreneurs

For entrepreneurs, securing essential funding and financing is pivotal in building a thriving business. Entrepreneurs can choose from various funding options that best suit their business objectives and financial needs. Here are several diverse alternatives for funding and financing. Whether you're a startup founder or an experienced business owner seeking expansion, comprehending these choices empowers you to make informed decisions and propel your entrepreneurial journey.

- Self-Financing

Self-financing, or bootstrapping, involves utilizing personal savings, credit, or assets to fund your business, providing complete control and ownership. It showcases your commitment and belief in your venture, instilling confidence in future investors. However, self-financing may constrain the speed and scale of growth while risking the depletion of personal funds or assets.

- Friends and Family

Raising funds from friends and family is a popular option for entrepreneurs. Supportive loved ones who share your vision may offer financial assistance. When seeking funding from this source, it's crucial to maintain professionalism, establish clear terms and expectations, and consider the potential impact on personal relationships.

- Crowdfunding

Crowdfunding has surged in popularity, empowering entrepreneurs to secure funds from a vast community of individuals. Some platforms enable entrepreneurs to present their ideas and gather contributions from interested backers. This method provides financial backing and serves as a marketing avenue, validating your business concept and cultivating an early adopter community. However, running a prosperous crowdfunding campaign demands meticulous planning, impactful marketing, and an enticing value proposition.

- Small Business Loans

Traditional small business loans from banks and financial institutions are popular financing options. They require a strong business plan, collateral, and credit history. Small business loans offer predictable repayment terms and help build a credit history. However, startups without a proven track record or substantial collateral may face loan challenges.

- Venture Capital

For ambitious high-growth startups, venture capital (VC) can be appealing. Venture Capital firms invest in early or growth-stage companies with great potential in return for equity. In addition to financial support, venture capitalists provide valuable expertise, industry connections, and mentorship. However, securing VC funding is competitive, demanding a solid business plan, scalable model, and compelling value proposition.

- Angel Investors

Angel investors, individuals, or groups who invest their capital in startups for equity fund ventures at an earlier stage than venture capital firms. They prioritize the entrepreneur's potential and the business concept. Angel investors provide valuable industry knowledge, mentorship, and connections. However, accessing angel funding necessitates a convincing pitch, a robust business plan, and a clear growth strategy, similar to venture capital.

- Grants and Government Programs

Government grants and programs fostering entrepreneurship and innovation present an alternative funding option. These initiatives offer financial assistance to businesses focused on specific sectors or objectives, often without equity dilution. Researching and applying for grants and government programs can significantly enhance your funding endeavors and enable you to leverage available resources effectively.

- Incubators and Accelerators

Incubators and accelerators are programs that support startups through mentorship, resources, and sometimes funding. They provide a structured environment for entrepreneurs to receive guidance, network, and access resources. Incubators nurture early-stage startups, helping them develop their ideas and strategies. Accelerators work with more advanced startups to accelerate their progress. Both offer funding, investor connections, and tailored support based on your business's needs.

- Strategic Partnerships

Strategic partnerships with established companies in your industry can provide access to funding and resources. Collaborating with strategic partners can offer financial support through joint ventures, licensing agreements, or shared investments. These partnerships also bring valuable expertise, market access, and credibility to your business, opening doors to new opportunities.

- Business Grants and Competitions

Many organizations and institutions offer business grants and competitions to support entrepreneurs. Grants can vary in size, ranging from modest sums to significant providing opportunities. However, they provide more than just financial support. Grants often come bundled with additional advantages such as mentorship, networking opportunities, and increased exposure for your business.

To tap into these benefits, conducting thorough research on local, regional, and industry-specific grants and competitions that align with your business objectives is crucial. By targeting grants tailored to your industry and business niche, you increase your chances of securing the funding and additional resources to propel your venture forward. Take the time to understand the eligibility criteria, application process, and deadlines for each grant or competition, and ensure that your application showcases how your business aligns with their specific requirements.

- Alternative Financing Options

In addition to the traditional funding sources mentioned above, entrepreneurs can explore alternative financing options. These include invoice financing, equipment leasing, revenue-based financing, and peer-to-peer lending. Alternative funding can be particularly beneficial for businesses with unique financial needs or those looking for flexible repayment terms. However, it's crucial to thoroughly evaluate the terms and fees associated with these options to ensure they align with your business's financial goals.

As you embark on your funding journey, it's essential to approach each option strategically. Tailor your approach to fit each funding source's specific requirements and expectations. Develop an effective business plan articulating your vision, market opportunity, and growth strategy. Prepare a polished pitch deck and practice your presentation to communicate your business's potential and value proposition effectively.

Building relationships and networking within the entrepreneurial ecosystem can significantly increase your chances of accessing funding. Attend industry events, join entrepreneurial communities, and actively seek mentorship from experienced entrepreneurs who can provide guidance and introduce you to potential investors or funding sources.

Remember that securing funding is not just about the money; it's about finding partners who align with your vision and can contribute to your business's long-term success. Evaluate the terms, consider the potential impact on your business's ownership and control, and ensure that your chosen funding aligns with your growth objectives.

There is a diverse range of funding and financing options available to entrepreneurs. You can confidently navigate the funding landscape by understanding each option's benefits, challenges, and best practices. Combine a comprehensive approach to your funding strategy, thorough preparation, and a clear value proposition to attract the right investors and secure the necessary capital to fuel your entrepreneurial journey. Remember, funding is just one piece of the puzzle, and building a solid business foundation, executing your plans effectively, and continuously iterating will ultimately determine the success of your venture.

The Pros And Cons Of Bootstrapping Vs. Seeking Outside Funding

Entrepreneurs often face a key decision between bootstrapping and seeking outside funding when starting or growing a business. Bootstrapping refers to using personal resources to fund a business, whereas seeking external funding involves acquiring capital from investors or lenders. Both approaches have advantages and disadvantages, so let's examine them in detail to assist you in making a well-informed choice.

❖ Bootstrapping

Pros:

1. Control and Ownership

Bootstrapping allows entrepreneurs to retain complete control and ownership of their businesses. You can make decisions without external investors, without compromising your vision or diluting your equity.

2. Flexibility and Agility

By self-funding, you can adapt and pivot your business strategy as needed. You can make quick decisions and respond to market changes without seeking approval from investors or adhering to their expectations.

3. Learning and Resourcefulness

Bootstrapping forces you to be resourceful and find creative solutions. It encourages you to deeply understand your business and its operations, fostering invaluable skills and knowledge.

4. Debt-Free Business

You don't accumulate debt or have monthly repayments by avoiding external funding. This can offer a sense of security and alleviate financial strain, particularly during the initial phases of your business endeavor.

Cons:

1. Limited Resources

Bootstrapping often means working with limited financial resources. This can restrict your ability to invest in growth initiatives, scale operations, or seize opportunities that require significant capital.

2. Slower Growth

With outside funding, your business may experience faster growth compared to ventures with substantial financial backing. Limited resources can constrain your ability to hire top talent, develop robust marketing campaigns, or expand into new markets.

3. Risk of Burnout

Bootstrapping often requires entrepreneurs to wear multiple hats and take on various responsibilities. This can lead to long working hours, increased stress, and the risk of burnout if not managed effectively.

❖ Seeking Outside Funding

Pros:

1. Access to Capital

Seeking outside funding provides:

- Access to a more substantial pool of capital.
- Enabling you to invest in critical areas such as product development.
- Marketing.
- Talent acquisition.

This infusion of funds can accelerate your business growth and expansion.

2. Expertise and Guidance

External investors often bring valuable expertise, industry knowledge, and networks. Their involvement can provide guidance, mentorship, and strategic insights that contribute to your business's success.

3. Validation and Credibility

Securing funding from reputable investors lends credibility to your business. It validates your concept, market potential, and growth prospects, making attracting customers, partners, and additional investment easier.

4. Shared Risk

By sharing the financial risk with investors, you can mitigate some personal liability that comes with solely relying on your resources. This can provide a safety net and reduce exposure to potential financial losses.

Cons:

1. Loss of Control

When seeking outside funding, you may need to give up a portion of ownership and decision-making authority. Investors may influence strategic decisions and frequently want a return on their investment, which reduces your autonomy.

2. Investor Expectations

External investors may have specific expectations regarding the growth and profitability of your business. This can create pressure to meet short-term targets or milestones, potentially diverting your attention from long-term strategic goals.

3. Dilution of Equity

Bringing in outside investors means diluting your equity. As you issue shares or ownership stakes, your ownership percentage decreases. This dilution can impact your control over the company's direction and potential future earnings.

4. Additional Responsibilities

Securing outside funding requires significant effort and time. You'll need to prepare pitches and presentations, conduct due diligence, negotiate terms, and manage ongoing investor relationships. These additional responsibilities can divert your focus from core business operations and require dedicated resources.

Choosing between bootstrapping and seeking outside funding is a critical decision that depends on your circumstances, goals, and risk tolerance. Bootstrapping allows for control, flexibility, and resourcefulness but may limit growth potential due to limited resources. On the other hand, seeking outside funding provides access to capital, expertise, and validation but comes with the trade-off of dilution of ownership and increased expectations from investors.

Ultimately, the best approach may involve a combination of both strategies. Many successful businesses start with bootstrapping in the early stages to prove their concept, build a customer base, and generate initial revenue. Seeking outside funding becomes an option if the business achieves a certain degree of stability and needs more money for expansion.

Regardless of your path, it's essential to carefully evaluate your financial needs, assess the potential risks and rewards, and align your decision with your long-term vision for your business. Seek advice from mentors, industry experts, and professionals in finance and entrepreneurship to gain valuable insights and make informed decisions.

Remember, funding is just one piece of the puzzle. Building a strong and sustainable business also requires a solid business plan, a clear value proposition, effective execution, and a focus on delivering value to customers. With a thoughtful approach to funding and a well-rounded business strategy, you can position your venture for success and achieve your entrepreneurial dreams.

How To Prepare For Investor Meetings And Pitches

Securing investment for your business is an exciting opportunity to take your venture to new heights. However, before you can secure that crucial funding, you need to impress potential investors with a compelling pitch. Investor meetings and pitches require careful preparation and an understanding of what investors seek. In order to increase your chances of success, here are some helpful preparation ideas for investor meetings and pitches.

1. Know Your Audience

Before meeting with investors, it's essential to research and understands their background, investment focus, and previous portfolio. This knowledge will help you tailor your pitch and align your business with their interests and investment criteria. Understanding your audience demonstrates professionalism and increases your credibility.

2. Refine Your Value Proposition

Your pitch is built around your value proposition. It is essential to describe your product or service's effectiveness in resolving issues, satisfying consumer needs, or providing value to customers. Highlight the unique features, benefits, and competitive advantages that differentiate your business. A strong value proposition will capture investors' attention and make your business stand out.

3. Develop a Compelling Story

Investors are interested in more than just numbers and data; they want to connect with your vision and the story behind your business. Create an engaging story that details your path, the issue you are addressing, and your motivation for starting your business. Weave in personal anecdotes, milestones, and any relevant achievements to engage investors on an emotional level.

4. Showcase Market Potential

Investors seek indications of growth and a significant market presence. To impress them, it is essential to demonstrate your awareness of the current market research, sector trends, and the size of the addressable market. Show that you have a thorough understanding of the target market, client segmentation, and the dynamics of the market. Utilize data and statistics effectively to substantiate your arguments and showcase a substantial opportunity for your organization.

5. Present a Clear Business Model

Investors must be able to see a path to profitability and a viable business model. Describe your revenue sources, pricing plan, and distribution methods. Explain how you plan to acquire and retain customers, demonstrate scalability, and showcase your plans for future growth. Investors are more likely to trust your business's sustainability and likelihood of long-term success if your business model is well stated.

6. Prepare Financial Projections

Investors want to understand the financial potential of your business. Prepare realistic and well-supported financial projections that demonstrate revenue growth, profitability, and cash flow. Include important indicators like customer lifetime value, acquisition cost, and estimated return on investment. Be ready to explain your assumptions in great detail and to take questioning.

7. Anticipate and Address Potential Concerns

It's critical to anticipate and aggressively address investors' queries or concerns. Make a thorough SWOT analysis (Strengths, Weaknesses, Opportunities, and Threats) to pinpoint potential risks and difficulties. Develop strategies and mitigation plans to address these concerns, showing investors you understand the potential obstacles and how to overcome them.

8. Practice and Refine Your Pitch

Rehearse your pitch multiple times to ensure you are confident, concise, and compelling. Practice with colleagues, mentors, or friends who can provide feedback and help you refine your presentation. Be mindful of your voice tone, posture, and overall presentational strategy. A polished and well-delivered pitch positively impacts investors.

9. Prepare a Strong Q&A Strategy

Investors will ask questions to gain deeper insights into your business. Anticipate common questions and prepare thoughtful and concise answers. Be transparent and honest about any limitations or challenges your business may face. If you need to know the answer, be upfront and offer to follow up later. Demonstrating your knowledge and ability to handle questions professionally builds trust with investors.

10. Follow-Up and Follow Through

After the investor meeting or pitch:

- Keep in mind to send a thank-you letter or email as a follow-up to show your appreciation for their consideration and time.
- Use this opportunity to reiterate key points from your pitch and address any additional questions or information they may have requested.
- Promptly provide any requested documents or data to demonstrate your professionalism and commitment.

11. Seek Feedback

Whether you secure investment or not, seeking feedback from investors is valuable. Ask for their thoughts on your pitch, areas for improvement, and any concerns they may have had. Constructive feedback can help refine your pitch and strengthen your business strategy for future opportunities. Embrace feedback as a learning opportunity and use it to iterate and improve.

12. Continuously Improve

Preparing for investor meetings and pitches is an iterative process. Take the lessons learned from each meeting and apply them to future pitches. Refine your pitch, update your financial projections, and adapt your strategy based on feedback and market insights. You will become more proficient at communicating the worth and potential of your company as you gain experience and a better understanding of investor expectations.

It is a crucial step in securing funding for your business. Following these tips diligently will increase your chances of success. Remember to seek feedback, continuously improve, and remain persistent in your pursuit of funding. With careful preparation and a compelling pitch, you can attract the right investors and take your business to new heights.

Leveraging Technology And Tools For Business Success

In today's fast-paced and interconnected world, leveraging technology and tools is essential for entrepreneurs to stay competitive and overcome challenges. From streamlining operations to enhancing productivity and reaching a wider audience, technology offers a plethora of opportunities for business success.

The following are how businesses can effectively leverage technology and tools to thrive in the modern landscape.

1. Streamlining Operations

Technology is crucial in streamlining business operations, reducing manual tasks, and increasing efficiency. Automation tools can automate repetitive processes, freeing up valuable time and resources. Project management software enables teams to collaborate seamlessly, track progress, and meet deadlines effectively. Inventory management systems help optimize stock levels, reduce waste, and improve inventory turnover. Businesses can streamline operations and focus on strategic initiatives using the right technology.

2. Enhancing Communication and Collaboration

Effective communication and collaboration are vital for business success. Technology provides many tools that facilitate communication and collaboration, regardless of physical location. Email, instant messaging, and video conferencing enable real-time communication and foster collaboration among remote teams. Cloud-based document-sharing platforms allow multiple stakeholders to work on documents simultaneously, ensuring version control and reducing delays. With these tools, businesses can foster effective communication and collaboration, increasing productivity and better decision-making.

3. Improving Customer Experience

Technology has transformed how businesses interact with customers, enabling personalized experiences and exceptional service. CRM (customer relationship management) solutions assist businesses in managing customer data, tracking interaction, and providing focused marketing campaigns. Customer support tools, such as chatbots and helpdesk software, enhance customer service by quickly and accurately responding to inquiries. E-commerce platforms enable businesses to create user-friendly online stores and offer seamless purchasing experiences. Proper leveraging of technology will enable businesses to deliver a superior customer experience and build strong relationships with their target audience.

4. Harnessing Data for Insights

Data has become a valuable business asset, providing insights into customer behavior, market trends, and operational efficiency. Analytical tools and business intelligence platforms help businesses collect, analyze, and visualize data to make informed decisions. Businesses can identify opportunities, optimize processes, and develop targeted strategies by harnessing data. Data-driven insights enable businesses to stay ahead of the competition, anticipate customer needs, and adapt quickly to changing market dynamics.

5. Embracing Digital Marketing

Digital marketing has completely changed how businesses advertise their goods and services. Online advertising platforms, social media marketing, and search engine optimization (SEO) techniques allow businesses to reach a wider audience and target specific demographics. Content management systems enable businesses to create and publish engaging content, enhancing brand visibility and customer engagement. Email marketing tools facilitate personalized and targeted communication with customers. Leveraging digital marketing tools will help businesses build a strong online presence, drive website traffic, and generate leads.

6. Ensuring Data Security

As businesses increasingly rely on technology, data security becomes a paramount concern. Cyber security tools and practices help businesses protect sensitive information, prevent data breaches, and maintain customer trust. Implementing robust firewalls, encryption methods, and multi-factor authentication enhances data security. Regular data backups and disaster recovery plans ensure business continuity in the event of a cyber-attack or system failure. Prioritizing data security will enable businesses to safeguard their reputation, protect customer data, and comply with privacy regulations.

Technology is a potent facilitator that may help businesses overcome obstacles, stimulate growth, and accomplish their objectives. Entrepreneurs can open up new opportunities and drive their companies toward long-term success by utilizing technology.

SERIES FIVE
HIRING AND MANAGING EMPLOYEES

Building a strong and cohesive team is crucial for the success of any business. Your employees play a vital role in driving growth and achieving your organizational goals. However, finding, retaining, and effectively managing top talent can be complex and challenging. In this series, we'll examine the crucial facets of hiring and managing employees, providing insightful advice to help you manage this crucial facet of your business.

Importance of Hiring Right

Building a high-performing team is vital for the long-term success of your business. Each employee brings unique skills, experience, and perspectives contributing to the organization's achievement. To ensure you hire the right individuals, it is crucial to establish a well-structured and thoughtful hiring process. By aligning candidates with your company's values, culture, and goals and selecting individuals with the right qualifications, cultural fit, and growth potential, you establish a solid foundation for a team that excels in performance and drives your business forward.

Techniques For Hiring And Managing Employee

- Creating an Effective Job Description

The initial step in attracting qualified candidates is creating a well-crafted job description. It should clearly and concisely outline the role, responsibilities, and necessary qualifications. By being specific about the desired skills, experience, and competencies, you can attract candidates who possess the desired qualities. Moreover, emphasize your company's mission, values, and unique selling points to entice individuals who align with your organizational culture.

- Implementing a Comprehensive Hiring Process

Establishing a comprehensive hiring process is crucial to make informed decisions and thoroughly evaluating candidates. This process may include multiple interview rounds, assessments, reference checks, and trial periods. Each step should assess the candidate's skills, qualifications, cultural fit, and potential for growth within your organization. By dedicating time and effort to the hiring process, you enhance the chances of finding the right individuals who can significantly contribute to the success of your business.

- Building a Diverse and Inclusive Team

Diversity and inclusion are crucial for cultivating innovation, creativity, and a positive work environment. You can create a team that brings many perspectives and ideas by actively seeking out candidates from diverse backgrounds, cultures, genders, and experiences. This diversity enables your business to approach challenges from various angles and connect with a broader customer base. Promoting an inclusive culture and providing equal opportunities for all employees to thrive and contribute to your organization's success is essential.

- Onboarding and Training

After successfully hiring new employees, ensuring a seamless onboarding and training process is vital. This phase helps them integrate into the team and establishes the tone for their interaction with the business. Provide them with the necessary knowledge, instruments, and resources to comprehend their responsibilities. Implement training initiatives that will improve their abilities and support their career development. Establishing a well-structured onboarding and training process will equip employees with the foundations for success and reinforce their dedication to the organization.

- Effective Communication and Feedback

Open and transparent communication is vital for creating a positive work environment and fostering productive relationships. Regularly communicate with your team, providing updates, sharing information, and encouraging their input. Actively listen to their feedback, concerns, and ideas, and address them promptly. Regularly receiving constructive feedback helps employees identify their areas of strength and growth, allowing them to set goals that are in accordance with the company's objectives.

- Promoting Employee Engagement and Recognition

Employee engagement is crucial for productivity, satisfaction, and retention. Foster a positive work culture by promoting collaboration, recognizing achievements, and creating opportunities for growth and development. Encourage teamwork, provide challenging assignments, and acknowledge employees' contributions. Implement reward and recognition programs to show your appreciation for their efforts. Engaged workers are more inclined to be motivated, devoted, and invested in the company's success.

- Managing Performance and Accountability

Effective performance management ensures employees understand their goals, receive regular feedback, and have clear expectations. Establish performance metrics and key indicators (KPIs) to measure individual and team progress. Regularly review performance, provide constructive feedback, and offer support for improvement. When employees are held responsible for their work, they embrace accountability and strive to deliver their utmost performance.

- Nurturing a Positive Work Culture

Establishing a positive work culture is crucial to enhance employee satisfaction and retention. Foster an environment that supports inclusivity and nurtures a culture of value, respect, and motivation for all employees. Encourage teamwork, collaboration, and open communication. Celebrate successes, promote work-life balance, and provide personal and professional growth opportunities. A positive work culture boosts morale, productivity, and overall job satisfaction.

- Resolving Conflicts and Challenges

Conflict is inevitable in any workplace, but how it is handled can make a significant difference. Encourage open dialogue and provide a safe space for employees to address conflicts or challenges. Act as a mediator when necessary, seeking fair and beneficial resolutions for all parties involved. Addressing conflicts promptly and effectively helps maintain a harmonious work environment and ensures that productivity and morale are not compromised.

- Supporting Employee Well-being

Prioritizing employee well-being is crucial for their overall satisfaction and productivity. Provide resources and support for maintaining physical and mental health. Offer flexible work arrangements, promote work-life balance, and encourage breaks and time off. Implement wellness initiatives and programs that encourage healthy habits and effective stress management.

Challenges Associated With Hiring And Managing Employees

Navigating the multifaceted realm of hiring and managing employees presents a mix of rewards and challenges for businesses, regardless of their scale. Building a formidable team is paramount to achieving success but necessitates addressing various obstacles. From sourcing the ideal talent to cultivating a positive work environment, entrepreneurs and managers must be equipped to tackle these challenges head-on, employing effective strategies to overcome them. By embracing these complexities and proactively addressing them, businesses can foster a thriving workforce and elevate their chances of attaining their goals.

Here are common challenges associated with hiring and managing employees and valuable insights to help entrepreneurs overcome them:

1. Attracting and Retaining Top Talent

One of the main hurdles businesses encounter is attracting and retaining exceptional talent. In a fiercely competitive job market, locating skilled individuals who align with your company's values and objectives can be daunting. Effective recruitment strategies attract high-quality candidates. Once hired, retaining talented employees requires offering competitive compensation, providing growth opportunities, and fostering a supportive work environment.

2. Cultural Fit and Team Dynamics

Ensuring cultural fit within the organization is vital for maintaining a cohesive and harmonious team. Hiring individuals who align with your company's values, vision, and work culture is crucial to foster collaboration and teamwork. However, achieving the right balance between cultural fit and diversity can be challenging. Striking a balance that values diverse perspectives while maintaining a shared sense of purpose requires careful consideration and effective communication.

3. Effective Onboarding and Training

Integrating new hires into the organization seamlessly is another challenge faced by businesses. Comprehensive onboarding programs that familiarize employees with company policies, procedures, and roles are essential for their success and job satisfaction. Additionally, ongoing training and development opportunities help employees enhance their skills and stay motivated. However, designing and implementing effective onboarding and training programs that meet the diverse needs of employees can be a complex task.

4. Communication and Collaboration

Effective communication and collaboration are fundamental for a productive and harmonious work environment. However, miscommunication, lack of transparency, and poor collaboration can hinder employee productivity and morale. Overcoming communication challenges requires implementing open lines of communication, encouraging feedback, and promoting a culture of transparency. Regular team meetings, clear expectations, and utilizing collaboration tools can foster effective communication and strengthen teamwork.

5. Performance Management and Motivation

Managing employee performance and keeping them motivated can be a significant challenge. Setting clear performance expectations, providing regular feedback, and recognizing achievements is essential for employee engagement. However, identifying and addressing performance issues constructively can be sensitive. Implementing performance management systems that encourage ongoing feedback, coaching, and development plans can help address performance challenges effectively.

6. Conflict Resolution

Conflict is inevitable in any workplace, and effectively resolving it is crucial for maintaining a healthy work environment. Addressing conflicts promptly, providing mediation when necessary, and fostering open communication are essential steps in conflict resolution. Building a culture that encourages respectful dialogue and offering conflict resolution training to managers can help mitigate conflicts and promote a positive work environment.

7. Compliance with Employment Laws and Regulations

Staying compliant with ever-changing employment laws and regulations is a significant challenge for businesses. Employers must navigate a complex legal landscape from hiring practices to payroll management and benefits administration. Seeking legal counsel, staying updated on employment regulations, and implementing robust HR policies and procedures can help mitigate legal risks and ensure compliance.

8. Employee Well-being and Work-Life Balance

Promoting employee well-being and work-life balance is increasingly recognized as essential for employee satisfaction and productivity. Balancing work and personal life demands can be challenging for employees, leading to burnout and decreased motivation. Offering flexible work arrangements, promoting a healthy work culture, and encouraging self-care can enhance employee well-being and performance.

Hiring and managing employees presents its own challenges; however, through meticulous planning and proactive strategies, businesses can effectively overcome these obstacles. Entrepreneurs can create a positive and productive work environment by addressing these challenges.

Strategies For Fostering A Positive Work Culture

Developing and nurturing a positive work culture is indispensable to achieving entrepreneurial success. It transcends the mere presence of employees working in unison. A positive work culture cultivates an environment of collaboration, active engagement, and a collective sense of purpose among team members. As a result, this amplifies productivity, improves employee satisfaction, and plays a pivotal role in the overall success and prosperity of the business. To foster a positive work culture, consider implementing the following strategies that promote harmony and well-being within the organization.

- Clear Communication

Establishing a positive work culture begins with open and transparent communication. Establish a setting that encourages team members to communicate freely, listen intently, and exchange feedback. Ensure that information flows freely across all levels of the organization, keeping everyone informed and aligned. Regularly communicate goals, expectations, and progress updates to promote clarity and avoid misunderstandings.

- Trust and Empowerment

Enable staff to take responsibility for their job and make decisions to create a culture of trust. Trust their expertise and provide them with the necessary resources and support to succeed. Encourage autonomy and delegate responsibilities, allowing employees to showcase their skills and contribute meaningfully to the organization.

- Recognition and Appreciation

Acknowledge and value the efforts and accomplishments of your team members. Celebrate important milestones, recognize exceptional performance, and offer constructive feedback as a means of appreciation. Show genuine appreciation for their contributions, both publicly and privately. This fosters a positive and motivating environment where employees feel valued and motivated to excel.

- Work-Life Balance

Promote a healthy work-life balance to support employee well-being and prevent burnout. Encourage employees to prioritize self-care, set boundaries, and balance work and personal life. Offer flexible work arrangements when possible and provide resources for stress management and work-life integration.

- Professional Development

Make the growth and development of your employees a priority by dedicating resources to their continuous learning and skill enhancement. Offer opportunities for training and provide resources for personal and professional goal setting. By supporting their aspirations, you enhance their capabilities and showcase your dedication to their long-term success.

- Collaboration and Team Building

Foster a collaborative work environment where teamwork and cooperation are valued. Encourage cross-departmental collaboration, promote knowledge sharing, and create opportunities for team-building activities. This strengthens relationships, boosts morale, and improves overall productivity.

- Clear Values and Purpose

Define and communicate the core values and purpose of your organization. Ensure that all employees understand and align with these values. Incorporate them into the day-to-day operations and decision-making processes. A shared sense of purpose creates a cohesive work culture and motivates employees to work towards common goals.

- Work Environment

Create a positive physical work environment that is conducive to productivity and well-being. Provide comfortable and functional workspaces, access to necessary tools and technology, and amenities that support employee comfort. Foster a clean, organized, and aesthetically pleasing atmosphere that promotes focus and creativity.

- Lead by Example

As an entrepreneur and leader, your actions and behavior set the tone for the work culture. Set a leading example by embodying the values and principles you desire to see in your employees. Demonstrate integrity, empathy, and professionalism in every interaction you have. Showcase a resilient work ethic and a steadfast dedication to both the prosperity of the business and the well-being of your employees.

A positive work culture not only attracts and retains top talent but also fosters innovation and collaboration and ultimately contributes to the success and growth of the business. Implementing these strategies will greatly assist entrepreneurs in fostering a positive work culture that nurtures employee engagement, satisfaction, and productivity.

SERIES SIX
LEGAL AND TAXATION

In entrepreneurship, where innovative ideas and unwavering passion drive the establishment of new enterprises, it is crucial to recognize the vital role of legal and taxation matters in ensuring your venture's success and long-term sustainability. A comprehensive comprehension and adept navigation of the legal and tax terrain are indispensable for safeguarding your business, adhering to regulatory frameworks, and optimizing your financial assets. By grasping the intricacies of these realms, you can secure a solid foundation for your business's prosperity and sustainable growth.

Although legal and taxation matters may not possess the allure of entrepreneurship, their significance cannot be overstated when securing your business's enduring success and expansion. This series aims to empower you with the essential knowledge and resources required to navigate the intricacies of legal complexities and make well-informed decisions that harmonize with your business objectives. By comprehending the legal and taxation landscape, you can preemptively tackle potential obstacles and lay a sturdy groundwork for your entrepreneurial odyssey.

Legal Considerations For Entrepreneurs, Including Business Registration And Incorporation

Legal considerations are vital for entrepreneurs as they begin their business journey. Understanding the legal landscape, complying with regulations, and addressing business registration and incorporation are crucial for establishing a strong foundation.

Benefits of Business Registration

Business registration is a critical step in establishing the legal identity of your enterprise. It offers numerous benefits, including:

❖ Legal Recognition

Registering your business grants it legal recognition and distinguishes it as a separate entity from yourself as an individual. This separation protects personal assets in case of business-related liabilities.

❖ Building Trust and Credibility

Registered businesses inspire trust and confidence among customers, suppliers, and potential partners. It demonstrates professionalism and a commitment to compliance with legal requirements.

❖ Access to Financing and Resources

Registering your business can enhance your access to financing options, such as business loans or grants. It also opens doors to resources, networks, and government programs to support registered enterprises.

Business Registration Process

The procedure for registering your business may vary depending on your location and the chosen legal structure. However, there are several common steps to take into consideration:

Step 1: Choose a Business Name

Select a unique and memorable name for your business that aligns with your brand identity. It is crucial to undertake extensive research before settling on the name of your business to confirm that it is not already in use and to carefully look into any potential trademark conflicts that might be connected to it.

Step 2: Determine the Legal Structure

Choose the business legal structure that best suits it, such as a corporation, partnership, limited liability company (LLC), or sole proprietorship. Each structure carries its implications concerning liability, taxation, and governance.

Step 3: Register with the Government Authorities

Ensure your business is registered with the relevant government agencies by researching the unique registration requirements in your jurisdiction. This typically involves filing the necessary forms, providing relevant information, and paying the required fees.

Step 4: Obtain Licenses and Permits

Depending on your industry and area, you should get licenses and permits to conduct business legally. These could include general business licenses, professional licenses, health permits, or zoning permits. Conduct thorough research to identify the necessary permits and complete the application process.

Incorporation

Incorporating your business furthers legal protection by establishing it as a separate legal entity. This process is typically more complex than business registration and offers additional benefits:

- Limited Liability Protection

Incorporating your business provides personal liability protection. In the event of financial obligations or legal disputes, your assets are generally safeguarded from being used to satisfy business-related debts.

- Enhancing Credibility and Professionalism

Incorporating your business adds credibility and professionalism, signaling your commitment to your venture.

This enhances your ability to attract potential investors, partners, and customers who recognize your seriousness and dedication.

- Tax Advantages

Various legal structures provide different tax advantages. It is a good idea to obtain advice from a tax adviser to fully understand the tax repercussions of incorporating your firm and choose the structure that best fits your financial goals.

- Access to Capital

Incorporation can facilitate access to capital through equity financing, allowing you to issue stock shares to investors. This can be particularly beneficial when seeking funding for growth and expansion.

❖ Perpetual Existence

An incorporated business can exist perpetually as a separate legal entity, even if ownership or management changes. This provides stability and continuity for the long-term success of your enterprise.

Seek Legal Assistance

Navigating the legal requirements of business registration and incorporation can be complex. Seeking legal assistance is recommended to ensure compliance and make well-informed decisions. An experienced business attorney can offer guidance throughout the process, review legal documents, and provide valuable, tailored advice to meet your needs.

By prioritizing legal considerations, entrepreneurs can establish a strong legal foundation for their ventures, mitigate risks, and ensure compliance with regulations. Adhering to the legal requirements protects your business, instills stakeholder confidence, and positions your enterprise for long-term success.

Taxation Laws And Compliance Requirements For Entrepreneurs

Taxation laws and compliance requirements are crucial aspects that entrepreneurs must consider when starting and running a business. Understanding the tax obligations and ensuring compliance with the relevant tax laws is essential to avoid penalties, maintain financial stability, and foster the long-term success of your venture. Let's explore the key taxation laws and compliance requirements for entrepreneurs.

- Business Structure and Tax Classification

The first step in understanding taxation laws is determining the appropriate business structure and tax classification for your venture. The prevalent business structures comprise sole proprietorship, partnership, limited liability company (LLC), and corporation. Each structure has different tax implications, such as self-employment taxes for sole proprietors, pass-through taxation for partnerships and LLCs, and corporate taxation for corporations. Seek guidance from a tax advisor or accountant to determine the most suitable business structure that aligns with your specific tax objectives.

- Federal Tax Obligations

Entrepreneurs must fulfill federal tax obligations to the Internal Revenue Service (IRS). This includes filing an annual tax return, reporting business income, and paying applicable taxes. The specific forms and requirements depend on your business structure. For example, sole proprietors report business income on Schedule C of their tax returns, while corporations must file a separate corporate tax return (Form 1120). Familiarize yourself with the IRS guidelines and deadlines to ensure timely and accurate tax filings.

- State and Local Taxes

In addition to federal taxes, entrepreneurs are also subject to state and local taxes. These taxes vary based on jurisdiction and may include income, sales, property, and payroll taxes. Research the specific tax requirements in your state and locality to understand your obligations and ensure compliance. Consider consulting with a tax professional familiar with your jurisdiction's laws to effectively navigate state and local tax obligations.

- Employment Taxes

When you have employees, adhering to employment tax obligations is essential. This requires correctly deducting and remitting payroll taxes such as Social Security, Medicare, and federal income tax from employee paychecks. Additionally, you are responsible for paying the employer portion of these taxes. Familiarize yourself with payroll tax withholding, reporting, and depositing requirements to ensure compliance with employment tax obligations.

- Sales and Use Taxes

You could be obligated to collect and send sales tax to the proper tax authorities if your business sells goods or services. Sales tax requirements vary by jurisdiction, and it is essential to understand the rules and rates applicable to your business. Consider whether your business operates in multiple states, which may trigger additional sales tax obligations. Implement proper systems to track and remit sales tax to avoid penalties and ensure compliance.

- Tax Deductions and Credits

Entrepreneurs should be aware of tax deductions and credits available to reduce their tax liability. Deductions refer to expenses that can be subtracted from your business income, reducing your taxable income. Typical deductions include business expenses like rent, utilities, supplies, and marketing costs. On the other hand, tax credits directly reduce your tax liability. Research and consult a tax professional to identify eligible deductions and credits to maximize your tax savings.

- Record Keeping and Documentation

Maintaining accurate and organized records is crucial for tax compliance. Keep detailed records of your business transactions, expenses, sales, and financial statements. This includes receipts, invoices, bank statements, payroll records, and tax filings. Effective record-keeping ensures that you have the necessary documentation to support your tax filings, respond to tax audits, and claim deductions or credits when necessary.

Seek Experts' Advice

Navigating the complexities of taxation laws can be challenging for entrepreneurs. Seeking guidance from a qualified tax advisor or accountant is strongly advised. They can provide expert assistance with tax planning, offer insights into specific tax laws and requirements, assist in devising tax planning strategies, and ensure compliance with tax regulations. A tax professional can also help you capitalize on applicable tax incentives, deductions, or credits that may benefit your business.

Protecting Your Intellectual Property Rights

Intellectual property (IP) is vital for businesses across various sectors. It encompasses original creations and expressions of the mind that can significantly contribute to your success. Regardless of your business type, whether in technology, consumer goods, or professional services, safeguarding your intellectual property, including trade secrets, is crucial. Protecting your IP should be an integral part of your business operations to maintain your competitive edge.

Neglecting to enforce and defend your intellectual property rights could lead to financial losses. To safeguard your intellectual property (IP), various laws such as trade dress, copyrights, patents, and trademarks provide legal protection that helps preserve the value of your intellectual assets.

Trade secrets

Trade secrets encompass valuable information, such as formulas, practices, processes, designs, instruments, patterns, or compilations that are not widely known or easily accessible. By leveraging trade secrets, businesses gain a competitive edge in the market. To maintain the status of a trade secret, companies must implement measures to safeguard the confidentiality of this information. Disclosing a trade secret exposes it to competitors, potentially compromising the company's market dominance and position.

How to Protect Your Trade Secrets

Ensuring the protection of your trade secrets necessitates obtaining signed confidentiality or non-disclosure agreements from employees, contractors, and other relevant parties involved. These agreements serve as a crucial measure to prevent the unauthorized disclosure of your trade secrets. Failing to establish such agreements may jeopardize the protection of your trade secrets and potentially waive their legal safeguards.

The trade dress law

Trade dress law safeguards the distinctive appearance or packaging of a product. It offers legal protection to trade dress through specific statutes. For trade dress to be eligible for protection, its identifiable features must clearly distinguish the product, as exemplified by the iconic Tiffany blue box. Additionally, these features should be nonfunctional, meaning they don't impact the product's cost, quality, or the manufacturer's competitive ability unrelated to reputation. Trade dress laws aim to shield consumers from unintentionally purchasing inferior goods or services due to confusingly similar trade dress associated with trusted brands.

Copyright laws

Copyright laws safeguard the tangible expression of creative works. They don't protect ideas themselves but rather the specific expression of those ideas. Once a work is created and fixed in a tangible form, it is automatically protected by copyright. Although copyright registration is not mandatory, it is recommended to register your copyright with the federal government to obtain optimal protection. Registering ensures the highest level of safeguarding and saves time in the event of an infringement lawsuit.

Patent rights

Patent rights entail exclusive state-granted rights to inventors for a defined duration in exchange for revealing their invention. These rights prohibit others from making, using, selling, or importing the patented invention. Acquiring a patent safeguards your distinct invention against infringement by external entities.

Trademark law

A trademark signifies the origin of goods or services through a word, phrase, or design. Trademark law, governed by state and federal statutes, protects trademarks. To secure your trademark, you can file a By filing "Intent to Use" application; you can protect your trademark concepts from the potential competition, especially if you have plans to utilize them in the future. Alternatively, if your business already utilizes a mark, you can file a "use-based" application to protect the intellectual property you employ for branding purposes.

The prosperity of your business relies on the strength of your intellectual property, be it proprietary technology or a cherished family recipe. Safeguarding your intellectual property is crucial to preserving your market share. By taking these essential steps, you can protect your intellectual property, avoiding litigation and enabling you to seek appropriate legal remedies to safeguard your business's interests.

Understanding Contracts And Agreements

Contracts and agreements are indispensable in business, facilitating clarity, protection, and shared understanding among parties. Whether launching a venture, forging partnerships, recruiting employees, or collaborating with clients and suppliers, a firm grasp of contracts is vital for safeguarding your interests and mitigating conflicts.

What are Contracts and Agreements?

Contracts and agreements serve as crucial legal instruments in business transactions. These binding documents delineate the rights, responsibilities, and obligations of involved parties while establishing the operational framework for a business relationship. They cover various aspects, such as the extent of work, payment arrangements, intellectual property ownership, confidentiality safeguards, dispute resolution mechanisms, and more. While verbal or written contracts are typically favored because they provide a comprehensive and unambiguous record of the agreed-upon terms and conditions.

Importance of Contracts and Agreements for Entrepreneurs

Contracts and agreements provide several key benefits for entrepreneurs:

1. Clarity and Communication

Contracts are essential for ensuring everyone involved knows their respective obligations and expectations. By precisely outlining the terms of the agreement, contracts help minimize misunderstandings and facilitate effective communication.

2. Protection of Rights

Contracts protect the rights and interests of all parties involved. They establish legal remedies in case of breach or non-performance, outline liability provisions, and address issues such as intellectual property ownership or confidential information.

3. Dispute Resolution

Contracts provide mechanisms for resolving disputes, including arbitration or mediation clauses. By addressing potential conflicts upfront, contracts help avoid costly and time-consuming legal battles.

4. Risk Management

Contracts allow entrepreneurs to identify and mitigate risks by including provisions that allocate risks and responsibilities between parties. They also outline insurance requirements and indemnification clauses to protect against potential losses.

Vital Elements of Contracts and Agreements

Understanding these essential elements of contracts and agreements is crucial for entrepreneurs:

❖ Offer and Acceptance

A contract begins with one party's offer and acceptance by the other. The offer should be clear, specific, and include all essential terms, while the acceptance should be unambiguous and communicated in a manner specified in the contract.

❖ Consideration

Contracts require a "consideration" or value exchanged between the parties. This can be money, goods, services, or promises to perform specific actions.

❖ Legal Capacity

It is necessary that each party to a contract be of legal age to do so for it to be enforceable. You must be of legal age, mentally sound, and free from compulsion or duress to qualify.

- ❖ Mutual Consent

To ensure the validity of a contract, it is crucial that both parties actively agree to its terms and conditions. This entails ensuring that all individuals involved in the transaction are fully aware of and in consensus with the contractual provisions and circumstances.

- ❖ Legality

Contracts must be lawful and comply with applicable laws and regulations. Any contract that involves illegal activities or violates public policy is considered void and unenforceable.

Given the complexity of contracts and agreements, it is highly recommended that entrepreneurs seek professional advice from lawyers specializing in contract law. An experienced attorney can help draft, review, and negotiate contracts to ensure they protect your interests and comply with relevant laws and regulations.

Understanding contracts and agreements is vital for entrepreneurs to establish clear and mutually beneficial business relationships. By properly comprehending the importance of contracts and the key elements involved and seeking professional advice when necessary, entrepreneurs can safeguard their interests, minimize risks, and foster successful business partnerships. Remember, contracts are the foundation of legal relationships, and taking a proactive approach to understanding and managing them will contribute to the long-term success of your entrepreneurial journey.

SERIES SEVEN
MARKETING AND SALES

Marketing and sales are two related yet distinct concepts essential for business success. While they have different roles, it's crucial to recognize their interdependence. Marketing primarily aims to attract and retain customers, while sales focus on the actual selling process. However, these functions rely on each other for optimal outcomes. A well-designed marketing strategy provides a foundation for successful sales, while the sales team's feedback and insights inform and enhance marketing efforts. Businesses can maximize their efficacy and promote sustainable growth by comprehending the connection between marketing and sales.

Let's draw a parallel to a sports team to grasp marketing and sales dynamics. In this analogy, marketing professionals act as coaches, while salespeople take on the role of athletes. Just like a seasoned coach, a successful marketing manager brings experience and expertise, having honed their skills through effective strategies. This expertise may come from working with various products and teams in previous organizations.

The marketing manager's role is to apply their expertise and tailor it to the specific products, people, and organizations they work with. Similar to a coach adapting strategies to their athletes' strengths and weaknesses, the marketing manager must customize their approach to the unique characteristics of their products and target audience.

Drawing from their experiences, the marketing manager guides and supports the sales team, much like a coach trains their athletes. By leveraging their insights and knowledge, the marketing manager shapes the overall marketing strategy, empowering the sales team to promote and sell the products effectively.

It's crucial to acknowledge that the sales team, despite the valuable expertise of the marketing manager, holds a pivotal position. They engage directly with customers and finalize deals, akin to athletes executing the coach's strategies. The sales team depends on the marketing manager's insights to align their efforts with marketing objectives.

The ultimate goal in this analogy is the overall success of the team. The marketing manager's expertise and strategies are instrumental in driving the sales team's accomplishments, helping them reach their targets and generate revenue. Through collaborative efforts and utilizing their skills, the marketing and sales functions establish a potent synergy that contributes to the overall prosperity of the business.

Understanding and acknowledging this synergy between marketing and sales allows businesses to develop a unified approach that optimizes customer acquisition, conversion, and retention. It enables the creation of a seamless and coordinated strategy that maximizes the effectiveness of both functions, leading to enhanced business outcomes.

Whether you're a new entrepreneur starting a business or an experienced business owner aiming to broaden your market, understanding the importance of effective marketing and sales strategies is crucial. These strategies serve as the foundation of your business, enabling you to attract and retain customers, generate revenue growth, and establish a strong brand identity. This series will explore the intricacies of developing successful marketing and sales strategies, providing you with the necessary knowledge and tools to drive your business toward tremendous success.

Developing A Marketing Strategy

Businesses looking to increase sales, brand recognition, and client attraction must have a solid marketing strategy. A carefully designed strategy acts as a roadmap, directing your efforts and ensuring that your marketing initiatives align with your business objectives. It's worth noting that an effective marketing strategy doesn't demand excessive time or expenses, so prioritize its development for your business's success.

If you seek greater certainty or encounter obstacles in formulating strong and influential marketing strategies to propel the growth and success of your business, consider leveraging the following valuable marketing tips to provide assistance.

1. Define Your Target Audience

Establishing a marketing strategy begins with determining your target audience. Having this insight will enable you to target your marketing efforts and select the best distribution methods for your target market.

2. Identify customer needs

Your prime focus should be on the needs and wants of your customers. Attempting to cater to the needs and wants of everyone is impractical, so it is crucial to identify your specific customer base and concentrate your marketing messages to generate the maximum impact among them. You should fully understand the market environment and assess your competitors. This will help you to ensure a strong market orientation for your business.

3. Communicate a clear idea of your business

Your business can prosper, but only if your market clearly understands your business. Ensure that your pamphlets and advertisements clearly and concisely describe your goods and services while being presented professionally. Having a comprehensive understanding of your company's capabilities and offerings is crucial for potential customers.

4. Conduct Market Research

Thorough market research is essential for understanding your industry, competitors, and market trends. Analyze your competitors' strategies, identify gaps in the market, and uncover opportunities for differentiation. By gaining insights into your target market's preferences and behaviors, you can develop strategies that effectively engage and resonate with your audience.

5. Develop a Unique Value Proposition

A strong value proposition sets your business apart from the competition. Clearly articulate your product or service's unique benefits and value to customers. Highlight what makes your offering special and how it addresses your customers' pain points. This will form the foundation of your marketing messaging.

6. Choose Effective Marketing Channels

Determine the most suitable marketing channels to reach your target audience. Think about online and offline platforms, including social media, email marketing, print media, events, public relations, search engine optimization (SEO), and paid advertising. Choose the channels based on the tastes and actions of your audience.

7. Create Compelling Content

At the core of every prosperous marketing strategy lies valuable content. Create high-quality, pertinent, captivating content that educates, entertains, or solves problems for your target audience. This can include blog posts, videos, infographics, podcasts, case studies, and whitepapers. Customize your content to align with each stage of the customer journey, fostering the growth of potential leads and cultivating brand loyalty.

8. Implement a Consistent Branding Strategy

Consistent branding is the key to building recognition and trust. Develop brand guidelines encompassing your logo, colors, typography, tone of voice, and visual elements. Maintain consistent brand representation across all marketing materials, including your website, social media profiles, and offline collateral, to ensure a cohesive and unified brand identity.

9. Keep in contact

You must regularly contact your consumers once you have created a good market. Let the consumers know about the latest updates, promotional offers, or some added features on your new products. You can do this through emails, phones, ads, etc. People love service.

10. Adapt and Refine

A marketing strategy should be flexible. Constantly monitor market trends, consumer behavior, and competitors' activities. Be ready to adapt and refine your strategies based on the insights and feedback you gather, ensuring their relevance and effectiveness.

Stay agile and responsive to ensure your marketing efforts remain effective and relevant. A marketing strategy must be continually developed, which calls for meticulous planning, innovation, and adaptability. You can create a solid marketing plan that promotes the expansion and success of your business by paying attention to and putting these suggestions into practice. In order to outperform your competitors and meet the evolving needs of your customers, it is crucial to evaluate and enhance your strategy consistently.

Importance Of Marketing And Sales For Entrepreneurs

The sales and marketing departments are essential pillars of organizational success, working together to bridge the divide between customer requirements and the products or services provided by the organization. Let's explore how sales and marketing contribute to entrepreneurial success and address common challenges entrepreneurs face.

- Market Research and Customer Insights

The sales and marketing teams are instrumental in conducting market research and acquiring valuable customer insights. They analyze market trends, identify target audiences, and understand customer needs and preferences. Thorough market research helps entrepreneurs to gain valuable insights that guide their product development, pricing strategies, and overall business approach. This information helps entrepreneurs make informed decisions, adapt to market changes, and create solutions that meet customer demands.

- Building Brand Awareness and Credibility

Effective marketing strategies are instrumental in building brand awareness and credibility for an entrepreneur's products or services. Through targeted marketing campaigns, entrepreneurs can create brand messaging that resonates with their target audience, effectively communicates the unique value proposition, and establishes credibility in the market. Through a strong brand presence, entrepreneurs can differentiate themselves from competitors and gain customer trust, leading to increased sales and market share.

- Lead Generation and Conversion

Sales and marketing teams work hand-in-hand to generate leads and convert them into customers. Marketing initiatives, including content marketing, social media advertising, and search engine optimization, attract potential customers and generate leads. Subsequently, the sales team follows up on these leads, fosters relationships, and guides prospects through the sales funnel. Entrepreneurs can optimize lead generation and conversion rates and ultimately drive business growth with effective sales and marketing strategies,

- Customer Relationship Management

Maintaining strong customer relationships is essential for long-term business success. Sales and marketing teams play a key role in nurturing customer relationships, ensuring customer satisfaction, and fostering loyalty. Entrepreneurs can build strong customer relationships through personalized marketing communications, excellent customer service, and ongoing engagement. This leads to repeat business and generates positive word-of-mouth referrals, which is invaluable for entrepreneurial growth.

- Adapting to Market Changes

The business landscape constantly evolves, and entrepreneurs must adapt to stay competitive. To identify new opportunities and potential challenges, sales and marketing teams monitor market trends, customer behaviors, and industry developments. By staying informed, entrepreneurs can proactively adjust their sales and marketing strategies, pivot their business approach, and seize emerging market opportunities. Embracing agility empowers entrepreneurs to outpace competitors and maintain relevance in a dynamic marketplace.

- Measuring and Analyzing Performance

Sales and marketing teams rely on data and analytics to measure the effectiveness of their strategies and campaigns. By tracking key performance indicators (KPIs) like sales revenue, client acquisition expenses, conversion rates, and customer satisfaction levels, business owners can obtain important insights into the efficacy of their sales and marketing operations. This data-driven approach allows entrepreneurs to identify areas for improvement, optimize their strategies, and make data-backed decisions to drive business growth.

The sales and marketing functions are crucial to entrepreneurial success. Entrepreneurs can harness sales and marketing power to strategically position their products or services, gain a competitive advantage, and propel business growth in a dynamic marketplace.

Creating A Brand And Brand Identity

Creating a powerful brand and establishing an engaging brand identity are vital for entrepreneurial triumph. A well-defined brand sets your business apart, fosters customer trust and loyalty, and differentiates you from competitors, leading to long-term business growth.

Difference Between Brand And Brand Identity

The distinction between brand and brand identity lies in their respective meanings. The brand represents people's overall perception and emotional response towards your business, encompassing every interaction and touch point. On the other hand, brand identity specifically pertains to the visual aspects that shape how your brand is visually perceived. It encompasses elements such as design, logo, and visual representation.

Importance of Brand and Brand Identity for Entrepreneurial Success:

❖ Standing Out

In a saturated market, a robust brand sets your business apart. It communicates the unique qualities of your offerings and convinces customers to choose you over competitors. By defining your brand clearly, you establish a distinctive identity that connects with your target audience, enabling you to shine in the marketplace.

❖ Building Trust

A strong brand cultivates trust and credibility with customers. When your brand is recognized and trusted, people are inclined to select your offerings and become loyal patrons. Consistency in your brand identity, which reflects your values, commitments, and quality standards, instills customer confidence. This fosters enduring relationships and encourages repeat business.

❖ Fostering Emotional Bonds

A robust brand establishes an emotional connection with customers. By sharing your brand story, values, and messaging, you can evoke emotions that deeply resonate with your target audience. You can forge a meaningful relationship that transcends mere transactions by addressing their aspirations, desires, or challenges. This fosters loyalty and encourages customers to become advocates for your brand.

❖ Driving Business Expansion

A reputable and widely recognized brand has a profound impact on business growth. It attracts new customers and fosters customer loyalty, opening doors for expansion into untapped markets. A positive brand reputation also acts as a magnet for potential partnerships, collaborations, and investment opportunities, propelling further growth and advancement.

Core Elements Of A Brand Identity

The brand identity comprises visual elements that work together as a cohesive system. The effectiveness of this system lies in its ability to create a visual language that is easily understandable to customers, enabling the business to communicate its message and values effectively.

Achieving mastery of the individual core elements is crucial when designing an identity. This mastery enables the elements to be seamlessly combined, creating a powerful visual language for your business. The success of the brand identity hinges on the consistency and quality of these elements and their skillful utilization.

Approach To Designing A Brand

It is crucial to understand the commercial and academic reasons behind a strong brand and its structure. Often, businesses and designers make choices solely driven by aesthetic preferences, neglecting strategic considerations. Similarly, some businesses make branding decisions based on personal taste rather than considering the preferences and needs of their target market. It is essential to align your brand choices with both commercial objectives and the expectations of your intended audience.

Strong brand design involves meticulously creating and harmonizing a brand's fundamental elements from its foundation. A critical aspect of the brand design process is to align the business's focus, allowing it to transform into a fully-fledged brand. Simplicity and clarity are vital for a brand to resonate with its target audience, providing effective navigation, building trust, and fostering meaningful connections in the market.

Steps to Create a Brand and Brand Identity:

Step 1: Define Your Brand Strategy

Start by clearly defining your brand strategy. Determine your target audience, brand positioning, key messages, and unique value proposition. Define your business's distinctive qualities and value propositions, and carefully shape the desired public perception of your brand.

Step 2: Conduct Market Research

Perform comprehensive market research to gain insights into your target audience's needs, preferences, and perceptions. Analyze market trends, study customer behaviors, and assess competitor strategies. This research will enable you to customize your brand identity and establish meaningful connections with your target audience.

Step 3: Develop Your Brand Story

Craft a compelling brand story communicating your purpose, mission, and values. Your brand story should resonate with your target audience and evoke an emotional response. Showcase the inspiration behind your business and how it positively impacts your customers' lives.

Step 4: Design Your Visual Identity

Develop a compelling visual identity that embodies your brand's personality and resonates with your intended audience. This encompasses designing a captivating logo, selecting an appropriate color palette, choosing fonts that align with your brand's image, and creating visually engaging assets that effectively communicate your brand essence. Ensure consistency across all touch points, including your website, packaging, marketing materials, and social media.

Step 5: Craft Your Brand Messaging

Develop clear and consistent messaging that communicates your brand value and resonates with your target audience. This includes defining your brand voice, tone, and key messages. Create catchy taglines, mission statements, and elevator pitches that effectively communicate the core and unique selling propositions of your business.

Step 6: Build Brand Awareness

Implement marketing and communication strategies to build brand awareness. Utilize various channels, such as social media, content marketing, advertising, and public relations, to create visibility for your brand. Engage with your audience, tell your brand story, and consistently communicate your brand values and offerings.

Step 7: Foster Brand Consistency

Maintain brand consistency across all customer touch points. Ensure that your brand identity, messaging, and visual elements are consistently applied in every interaction with your audience. This consistency builds trust, reinforces brand recognition, and creates a cohesive brand experience.

Step 8: Protect Your Brand

Take steps to protect your brand legally. Trademark your brand name, logo, and other distinctive elements to prevent others from infringing upon your brand identity. Monitor online platforms and take prompt action against any misuse or misrepresentation of your brand.

By following these steps and consistently investing in your brand, you can create a powerful brand identity that resonates with your target audience, differentiates you from competitors, and contributes to the overall success of your entrepreneurial venture.

Common Marketing And Sales Challenges Faced By Entrepreneurs

Marketing and sales pose significant challenges for entrepreneurs. While these obstacles may differ based on industry and business models, certain challenges persist across the entrepreneurial landscape. Entrepreneurs must comprehend these challenges to devise effective strategies and navigate hurdles successfully. Here are some common marketing and sales challenges faced by entrepreneurs:

- Limited Budget

One of the most prevalent challenges for entrepreneurs is limited financial resources. Starting a business often requires careful budgeting, and allocating funds for marketing and sales activities can be challenging. Entrepreneurs must discover innovative and budget-friendly approaches to connect with their desired audience and market their offerings effectively.

- Building Brand Awareness

Developing brand recognition and trust is paramount for entrepreneurs, particularly in competitive markets. It requires dedicated time and effort to establish a recognizable and reputable brand. Entrepreneurs must develop a strong brand identity, engage in consistent messaging, and employ various marketing strategies to increase brand visibility and awareness among their target audience.

- Generating Leads and Converting Customers

Acquiring new customers is a common challenge faced by entrepreneurs. Generating leads and converting them into paying customers requires a well-defined marketing and sales strategy. Entrepreneurs need to implement effective lead-generation tactics, nurture relationships with prospects, and optimize their sales processes to improve conversion rates.

- Targeting the Right Audience

One of the primary obstacles entrepreneurs encounter is identifying and reaching their ideal audience. Picture launching a business in a location where the residents have no demand or inclination for the products or services you provide. Regardless of the excellence of your offerings, your business will face difficulties gaining traction if it fails to resonate with your target audience.

For instance, let's say you decide to open a surf shop in a landlocked city where there are no nearby beaches or surfing spots. Despite having a fantastic range of surfboards, wetsuits, and accessories, your target audience is virtually non-existent. The local community may have little to no interest in your products because they need to align with their needs or lifestyle. Entrepreneurs must conduct thorough market research to understand their target market's demographics, preferences, and needs. Failure to accurately identify the target audience can lead to wasted marketing efforts and resources.

- Competition and Market Saturation

Many industries are highly competitive, making it challenging for entrepreneurs to stand out. Market saturation can also make gaining market share and attracting customers easier. Entrepreneurs need to differentiate their products or services, highlight unique value propositions, and develop effective marketing strategies to overcome these challenges.

- Adapting to Technological Advancements

Technology plays a significant role in marketing and sales. For entrepreneurs, staying updated with technological advancements can be daunting, especially when resources are limited. The use of appropriate devices and platforms, knowledge of emerging technologies, and maximizing the power of digital marketing channels are all necessary for businesses to remain competitive in the digital age. By doing so, entrepreneurs can maximize their chances of success and effectively navigate the ever-changing digital landscape. With successful target audience engagement in the digital environment, businesses can stay ahead of the curve.

- Sales and Marketing Alignment

Keeping the sales and marketing departments in alignment can take time and effort. These divisions' inability to work together effectively, miscommunication, and competing goals can all impede business expansion. Entrepreneurs need to foster strong communication channels, establish shared goals, and promote cross-functional collaboration to maximize the impact of marketing and sales efforts.

- Measuring ROI and Performance

Determining the return on investment (ROI) and measuring the performance of marketing and sales activities can be complex. Entrepreneurs need to track key performance indicators (KPIs), analyze data, and implement effective measurement techniques to evaluate the effectiveness and success of their marketing campaigns. Understanding ROI helps allocate resources efficiently and make data-driven decisions.

- Scaling and Growth

Entrepreneurs face unique marketing and sales challenges to scale their businesses. Scaling requires adapting marketing strategies to accommodate a larger customer base, expanding into new markets, and managing increased demand. Entrepreneurs must develop scalable marketing and sales processes to support business growth effectively.

- Adapting to Market Changes

Entrepreneurs face a range of marketing and sales challenges on their journey to business success. Markets constantly evolve, and entrepreneurs must stay agile to adapt to changing market dynamics. Keeping up with consumer trends, industry shifts, and emerging market forces is essential. Entrepreneurs must be willing to pivot their marketing and sales strategies and embrace innovation to stay relevant and competitive. Understanding these challenges and implementing effective strategies will enable entrepreneurs to overcome obstacles, reach their target audience, and achieve sustainable growth.

SERIES EIGHT
SCALING AND GROWTH

Scaling and growth are pivotal stages in the life of a business, signifying the fruition of entrepreneurial endeavors and the pursuit of new horizons. It is an exciting phase where operations expand, revenue surges, and the customer base broadens. However, sustainable growth necessitates meticulous planning, strategic choices, and a steadfast commitment to scalability. Achieving long-term success involves carefully navigating these elements, ensuring optimal outcomes and enduring prosperity.

This series will explore the strategies, best practices, and challenges associated with scaling and growing your business. Whether you're an aspiring entrepreneur seeking to elevate your startup or an established business owner with expansion goals, this series offers invaluable insights and actionable tips to guide your business toward sustained success. With a focus on practical strategies, you'll gain the knowledge and tools necessary to propel your business forward and achieve your long-term objectives.

Strategies For Scaling And Growing Your Business

Embarking on scaling and growing your business is an exciting phase, filled with fresh prospects and obstacles. It serves as a testament to your unwavering commitment and entrepreneurial foresight. Nevertheless, strategic navigation is crucial at this stage to secure enduring growth and prosperity in the long run. Implementing effective strategies is pivotal in propelling your business toward successful scaling and expansion.

❖ Develop a Clear Vision and Strategy

Before embarking on the scaling journey, having a clear vision for your business is crucial. Define your goals, mission, and values. This will guide your strategic decisions and help you stay focused as you scale. Develop a growth strategy that outlines your target markets, product expansion plans, and operational improvements.

❖ Invest in Technology and Automation

Technology plays a vital role in scaling businesses. Identify areas where technology can streamline operations, enhance productivity, and improve customer experiences. To optimize your processes, consider implementing automation tools, customer relationship management (CRM) systems, and cloud-based solutions.

❖ Build a High-Performing Team

As your business expands, the importance of building a skilled and committed team cannot be overstated. When hiring, prioritize individuals who align with your company culture and possess the expertise and abilities to fuel growth. By assembling a team of competent and skilled individuals, you can establish a solid foundation for success and ensure the long-term endurance of your business. Provide ongoing training and development opportunities to nurture their talents. Foster a positive work environment that encourages collaboration, creativity, and innovation.

❖ Focus on Customer Experience

Customer satisfaction serves as the cornerstone for driving business growth. It is crucial to allocate resources toward comprehending the needs and preferences of your customers. You can continuously improve your products, services, and overall customer experience by actively seeking feedback, analyzing data, and leveraging customer insights. This customer-centric approach fosters loyalty and attracts new customers, propelling your business toward sustainable growth. Provide exceptional customer support and build long-term relationships to foster customer loyalty and advocacy.

❖ Expand Your Market Reach

Identify new market opportunities to expand your customer base. Conduct thorough market research to gain insights into the demand for your offerings across various regions and demographics. This will enable you to identify untapped opportunities and new target audiences. With this knowledge, you can create targeted marketing campaigns to reach and engage these new audiences effectively. Consider partnerships, collaborations, or joint ventures to access new markets more efficiently.

❖ Diversify Your Offerings

Introduce new products or services that complement your existing offerings. This allows you to tap into new revenue streams and attract a broader customer base. Conduct market analysis to identify gaps or emerging trends that align with your business capabilities. Continuously innovate and adapt your offerings to stay competitive in the market.

❖ Strengthen Your Brand

A powerful brand may set your business apart from rivals and draw in devoted clients. Spend money on branding initiatives to establish a strong brand identity. Develop a consistent brand voice, visual identity, and messaging across all customer touch points. Utilize channels for digital, social, and content marketing to promote brand awareness and interact with your target market.

❖ Monitor Key Performance Indicators (KPIs)

Establish KPIs that align with your growth objectives and track them regularly. Key metrics such as revenue growth, customer acquisition costs, customer lifetime value, and profitability can provide insights into the effectiveness of your scaling strategies. Use these metrics to make data-driven decisions and adjust your approach as needed.

- ❖ Foster Strategic Partnerships

Collaborating with other businesses can help accelerate your growth. Seek strategic alliances or collaborations with businesses with comparable target markets or complementary product lines. Through pooled resources, knowledge, and access to new markets, these alliances can promote both parties' success.

- ❖ Stay Agile and Adaptive

The business landscape is dynamic, and successful scaling requires agility and adaptability. Continuously monitor market trends, industry changes, and customer feedback. Be open to adjusting your strategies and embracing new opportunities. Stay innovative and responsive to evolving customer needs to maintain a competitive edge.

Remember, scaling and growing your business requires strategic planning, customer-centricity, investment in technology, and fostering a strong team. These strategies will position your business for sustainable growth and navigate the challenges that come.

Identifying Growth Opportunities And Challenges

In entrepreneurship's dynamic and rapidly changing realm, recognizing growth prospects and skillfully maneuvering through the accompanying hurdles are paramount for enduring triumph. Entrepreneurs incessantly endeavor to expand their enterprises, penetrate untapped markets, and enhance profitability. Nevertheless, the pursuit of growth is rife with obstacles. Gaining a comprehensive understanding of growth opportunities and effectively tackling the associated challenges can empower entrepreneurs to elevate their ventures to unprecedented levels of accomplishment.

The Importance of Identifying Growth Opportunities

1. Expanding Market Reach

Recognizing growth opportunities enables entrepreneurs to expand their reach and tap into new markets, effectively connecting with a broader customer base. By identifying untapped niches or emerging trends, entrepreneurs can strategically position themselves to meet the demands of these markets.

2. Increasing Revenue and Profitability

Growth opportunities often translate into increased revenue and profitability. Whether through product diversification, geographical expansion, or innovative business models, identifying and capitalizing on growth opportunities can significantly boost financial performance.

3. Enhancing Competitive Advantage

In a competitive landscape, growth opportunities allow entrepreneurs to differentiate themselves from rivals. By identifying unique selling propositions, leveraging innovation, and anticipating market trends, entrepreneurs can strengthen their competitive advantage and secure long-term success.

How to identify growth opportunities

1. Stay Updated on Industry Trends

Keep a careful watch on business-relevant market trends and technical developments. Attend industry conferences, workshops, and seminars to stay informed about the latest developments. This will enable you to spot emerging trends and adapt your business accordingly.

2. Explore New Market Segments

Look beyond your target market and explore new customer segments that could benefit from your products or services. Conduct market segmentation analysis to identify untapped demographics or niche markets that align with your offerings. By expanding your customer base, you can unlock new growth opportunities.

3. Innovate and Diversify

Develop an innovative culture within your company and empower staff to come up with innovative ideas. Constantly evaluate your product or service offerings and look for ways to enhance or diversify them. Innovating and introducing new offerings can attract customers, increase market share, and drive growth.

4. Assess Internal Capabilities

Evaluate your internal capabilities and resources to identify areas where you can leverage your strengths for growth. This may involve investing in employee training, upgrading technology infrastructure, or optimizing internal processes to enhance efficiency and productivity.

5. Collaborate and Partner

Seek collaborations and partnerships with complementary businesses or industry influencers. By joining forces, you can leverage each other's strengths, expand your reach, and access new customer segments. Partnerships can also lead to joint marketing initiatives, co-branding opportunities, and shared resources, all of which can contribute to growth.

Challenges in Pursuing Growth

- Resource Limitations

Scaling a business requires significant resources, including capital, workforce, and infrastructure. Many entrepreneurs need help securing adequate funding, hiring skilled talent, and establishing robust operational systems to support growth initiatives.

- Market Volatility and Uncertainty

In the ever-changing landscape of markets, entrepreneurs face the reality of dynamic and unpredictable conditions. Economic shifts, evolving consumer behaviors, and disruptive technologies present challenges entrepreneurs must navigate. The ability to adapt to these uncertainties while staying on track with growth objectives can be a daunting task.

- Operational Efficiency and Scalability

As businesses grow, maintaining operational efficiency becomes critical. Entrepreneurs must streamline processes, implement scalable systems, and optimize resource allocation for sustainable growth.

Strategies for Overcoming Growth Challenges

1. Comprehensive Business Planning

Developing a well-defined business plan that accounts for growth opportunities and addresses potential challenges is essential. A robust plan should include the following:

- A detailed market analysis.
- Growth projections.
- Risk mitigation strategies.
- An actionable timeline for execution.

2. Strategic Partnerships and Collaborations

Partnering with complementary businesses or forming strategic alliances can provide access to new markets, resources, and expertise. Collaborative efforts can help overcome resource limitations and accelerate growth.

3. Continuous Learning and Innovation

Entrepreneurs must foster a culture of continuous learning and innovation within their organizations. By staying updated on industry trends, investing in research and development, and encouraging creative thinking, entrepreneurs can adapt to changing market dynamics and stay ahead of the competition.

4. Scalable Infrastructure and Technology

Investing in scalable infrastructure and leveraging technology solutions is crucial for accommodating growth. Implementing robust operations, sales, and customer management systems can enhance efficiency and enable seamless scalability.

5. Talent Acquisition and Development

Building a high-performing team is essential for sustainable growth. Entrepreneurs should focus on attracting top talent, fostering a positive work culture, and investing in training and development programs to empower employees and drive organizational success.

Identifying growth opportunities and managing the accompanying challenges is fundamental to entrepreneurial success. However, growth comes with hurdles. Overcoming those challenges is critical to sustaining growth momentum. Adopting strategic approaches, fostering innovation, and building strong partnerships will effectively help entrepreneurs to position themselves for long-term success.

Scaling Challenges And How To Overcome Them

Scaling a business is both exhilarating and fulfilling, but it brings its fair share of challenges. Entrepreneurs face a multitude of obstacles as they endeavor to expand their operations and establish a stronger market presence. It is essential to comprehend these challenges and devise strategies to surmount them in order to achieve successful scaling. Let us examine the common challenges when scaling a business and explore effective approaches to overcome them.

1. Resource Management

One of the significant challenges of scaling is managing resources effectively. As your business grows, demands on your resources, such as finances, human capital, and infrastructure, increase. It's important to allocate resources strategically and ensure they are utilized optimally. Conduct a comprehensive evaluation of your resource requirements and pinpoint areas that may necessitate additional investments. Implementing robust systems and processes can help streamline operations and improve resource management.

2. Maintaining Quality

When expanding your business, it's essential to maintain the quality of your goods and services. Maintaining consistent quality and customer satisfaction can present challenges as your customer base grows. Prioritize training and development initiatives to equip your workers with the knowledge and abilities necessary to uphold quality standards to overcome this. Implement quality control measures and regularly monitor customer feedback to identify areas for improvement.

3. Scalable Infrastructure

Scaling your business requires a scalable infrastructure that can handle increased demand. This includes your physical infrastructure, such as production facilities or office space, as well as your technological infrastructure, including your website, e-commerce platform, and IT systems. Examine your current infrastructure and note any potential upgrades or expansions. Investing in scalable technologies and cloud-based solutions can help you adapt to changing needs and accommodate growth efficiently.

4. Market Competition

Scaling a business often means facing increased competition. New entrants may emerge, and existing competitors may step up their game. To overcome this challenge, focus on differentiation and innovation. Discover your distinctive selling propositions and adeptly convey them to your target audience. Stays updated on market trends and constantly seek ways to improve your products or services. Building strong customer relationships and delivering exceptional customer experiences can help you stand out.

5. Managing Cash Flow

Scaling requires significant investment, and managing cash flow becomes even more critical. Rapid growth can strain your cash flow, leading to financial challenges. To overcome this, develop a detailed financial plan and regularly monitor your cash flow. Explore financing options, such as business loans or lines of credit, to ensure you have access to capital when needed. Implement robust financial management practices, including budgeting, forecasting, and cost control measures.

Scaling a business comes with its share of hurdles. Yet these challenges can be conquered with meticulous planning and implementing impactful strategies. Embrace growth possibilities and continuously refine your approaches to stay ahead of the ever-changing landscape.

Preparing For Expansion

As your business reaches a certain stage of success, thoughts of expansion naturally arise. It's an exciting prospect, especially when sales are booming, and customers are satisfied. Your business is running smoothly on autopilot. This is when the desire to embark on new ventures and elevate your business to the next level intensifies. However, it's important to approach expansion opportunities with caution. While it may seem tempting to seize every opportunity that comes your way, hasty decision-making can have detrimental effects on your business. It is crucial to carefully evaluate any thoughts of business expansion carefully, considering the advantages and disadvantages involved.

Before embarking on business expansion plans, it is crucial to address the initial question: Can a market support your growth? Assessing whether you are entering an established and thriving market or venturing into unexplored territory is important. Both scenarios can present enticing opportunities, but ensuring that your product or service can viably meet the supply-demand gap in the market is essential. Understanding the market dynamics and the potential for your offerings to meet customer needs is key in determining the feasibility and success of your expansion endeavors.

Preparation For Expansion

During the growth journey of a business, this phase is of utmost importance. It necessitates meticulous planning, strategic decision-making, and the establishment of a strong foundation to facilitate a seamless transition into new markets, expanded production capabilities, or a wider customer base. By adequately preparing for expansion, entrepreneurs can position their businesses for long-term success and unlock their full growth potential.

Here are the key considerations and steps involved in preparing for expansion:

- Evaluate Market Opportunities

Before embarking on an expansion journey, assessing market opportunities and trends is crucial. Conduct market research to identify potential target markets, analyze consumer behavior, and understand the competitive landscape. By conducting this research, you will gain valuable insights into the market demand for your products or services, empowering you to make informed decisions regarding the most favorable locations and strategies for expansion.

- Develop a Growth Strategy

A well-defined growth strategy is essential for successful expansion. It outlines your goals, target markets, and the initiatives you will undertake to achieve them. Define your unique value proposition and competitive advantage in the new markets you plan to enter. Consider pricing, distribution channels, and marketing campaigns tailored to your target audience. A clear growth strategy will guide your actions and ensure alignment across the organization.

- Strengthen Your Team

As your business expands, you need a capable and motivated team to support your growth objectives. Assess your current workforce and identify any skill gaps that need to be filled. Hire talented individuals who align with your company culture and have the expertise required for the expansion phase. Invest in training and development programs to upskill your existing employees and empower them to take on new responsibilities.

- Secure Funding Options

Expansion often requires a significant financial investment. Evaluate your funding options and secure capital to support your growth plans. This may involve seeking external funding from investors, applying for business loans, or exploring government grants and incentives. Develop a robust financial plan that outlines your projected expenses, revenue forecasts, and cash flow projections to demonstrate the feasibility of your expansion to potential investors or lenders.

- Establish Financial Stability

Before expanding, it is crucial to ensure the financial stability of your business. Review your financial statements, including balance sheets, income, and cash flow statements, to assess your financial health. Identify any areas of concern and take necessary measures to improve profitability, reduce costs, and manage cash flow effectively. Implement robust financial management systems and processes to support the increased demands of the expanded operations.

- Mitigate Risks

The expansion comes with inherent risks, and it is essential to identify and mitigate them proactively. Conducting a comprehensive risk assessment enables you to proactively identify potential challenges and develop contingency plans to mitigate them effectively. By being prepared for various scenarios, you can enhance your business's resilience and ensure continuity in the face of unexpected events.

Consider factors such as market volatility, regulatory changes, supply chain disruptions, and increased competition. By anticipating and planning for potential risks, you can minimize their impact on your expansion efforts.

Various factors, including market demand, competitive landscape, and internal capabilities, influence the decision to expand a business. Expanding your business requires careful consideration, extensive planning, and a comprehensive understanding of the associated risks and potential benefits. It requires a clear vision, innovative thinking, and strategic implementation. Therefore, it is imperative to have all the essential elements before embarking on this transformative journey to maximize your chances of success.

SERIES NINE
MINDSET AND PERSONAL DEVELOPMENT

Business success extends beyond financial accomplishments. It encompasses personal development, mindset, and the capacity to establish a flourishing organization. The path of entrepreneurship demands discipline, perseverance, and a dedicated work ethic. You are a key player in every facet of your business as an entrepreneur, and how you respond to obstacles determines how successful you will be.

In the world of entrepreneurship, ongoing personal growth is paramount to thrive. Developing oneself mentally, emotionally, and physically is essential, as building a business often entails challenging circumstances that put these capabilities to the test. Thus, prioritizing self-improvement becomes an imperative task. The level of success you desire is directly proportional to the dedication and energy you devote to your personal development journey.

Entrepreneurship has a unique ability to uncover weaknesses and shed light on areas for improvement. Embracing this reality and directly addressing your weaknesses is crucial for attaining remarkable outcomes. Understand that personal development is a continuous journey that demands dedication and time. Don't be disheartened if immediate progress isn't apparent. Instead, enrich your mind with resources that fortify your mindset and seek guidance from fellow individuals on their self-improvement journeys.

As an entrepreneur, possessing patience and persistence is crucial for achieving success. Embrace a growth mindset and continuously strive to enhance your skills and knowledge. Surround yourself with positive, like-minded individuals who inspire and support your growth.

Navigating this entrepreneurial journey alone can be daunting. It's advantageous to align yourself with a system and leadership development programs that offer guidance and support. Plugging into these valuable resources significantly increases your chances of attaining your desired success.

This series will explore the crucial part that mindset plays in entrepreneurship success. We will explore the concept of a growth mindset and share effective strategies for conquering limiting beliefs. Recognizing your mindset's immense power and actively nurturing personal growth will pave the way for triumph in the business world.

Prepare to embark on a transformative self-investment and skill development journey essential for crafting a prosperous business. This series will equip you with invaluable insights, strategies, and motivation to propel you toward your entrepreneurial aspirations. Embrace the path of personal growth, and witness the simultaneous flourishing of your business. Unlock your boundless potential and manifest the success you envision as an entrepreneur.

The Role Of Mindset In Entrepreneurial Success

Entrepreneurial success is not solely reliant on external variables like market conditions or business tactics. The mindset and beliefs of individuals heavily influence it. How entrepreneurs think, interpret challenges, and seize opportunities can profoundly shape their chances of success. With that in mind, let's delve into the pivotal role of mindset in entrepreneurial endeavors and examine the essential components that foster a positive and growth-oriented mindset.

❖ Growth Mindset

A growth mindset is the foundation for entrepreneurial success. It is the belief that abilities and intelligence can be developed through dedication, effort, and continuous learning. Entrepreneurs with a growth mindset embrace challenges, view failures as learning opportunities, and persist in facing setbacks. They believe their skills and capabilities can be improved over time, allowing them to adapt and thrive in a dynamic business environment.

❖ Resilience and Perseverance

The journey of entrepreneurship is filled with obstacles and setbacks. It requires resilience and the ability to bounce back from failures and disappointments. Strong-minded business owners embrace setbacks as stepping stones to progress because they recognize that they are a necessary part of the process. They maintain a positive attitude, learn from their mistakes, and keep pushing forward despite challenges. Their perseverance enables them to navigate tough times and focus on their goals.

❖ Positive Self-Belief

Believing in oneself is crucial for entrepreneurial success. Entrepreneurs with a positive mindset have confidence in their abilities and their vision. They trust their instincts, make bold decisions, and take calculated risks. This self-belief allows them to overcome self-doubt and fear of failure. They understand that success starts from within and cultivate a strong sense of self-worth and confidence.

❖ Adaptability and Open-Mindedness

The business landscape constantly evolves, and successful entrepreneurs embrace change with an open mind. They are adaptable and flexible, willing to pivot their strategies and explore new opportunities. They seek feedback and input from others, recognizing that collaboration and diverse perspectives can lead to innovative solutions. By remaining open-minded, entrepreneurs can stay ahead of the curve and seize emerging trends and market shifts.

❖ Goal Setting and Vision

Entrepreneurs with a success-oriented mindset set clear goals and visualize their desired outcomes. They create a compelling vision for their business and constantly align their actions with that vision. They break down their goals into actionable steps and monitor their progress. Entrepreneurs may maintain concentration, motivation, and progress toward success by having a solid sense of direction and purpose.

❖ Continuous Learning

Successful entrepreneurs recognize the value of gaining new knowledge and abilities. Learning is a lifelong process. They invest in personal and professional development through formal education, mentorship, or self-study. They stay up-to-date with industry trends, market insights, and emerging technologies. Continuous expansion of their knowledge base will enable entrepreneurs to make informed decisions, innovate, and stay ahead of their competitors.

❖ Embracing Failure

The entrepreneurial journey will inevitably include failure. However, those with a growth mindset see failure as a valuable learning experience. They understand that failure is not the end but rather an opportunity to grow, refine their strategies, and come back stronger. They don't hesitate to take chances and see failures as a stepping stone to success. By embracing failure, entrepreneurs cultivate resilience, learn valuable lessons, and develop the tenacity to overcome future challenges.

The role of mindset in entrepreneurial success cannot be overstated. Developing a positive and growth-oriented mindset empowers entrepreneurs to navigate challenges, embrace opportunities, and achieve their goals. Entrepreneurs can reach their full potential and improve their chances of business success by developing a growth mindset.

Developing A Growth Mindset

To achieve success in the dynamic and challenging realm of entrepreneurship, cultivating a growth mindset is paramount. A growth mindset entails a firm conviction that you and your organization can continuously grow and improve, unhindered by obstacles.

Developing an entrepreneurial growth mindset involves adopting a mindset that embraces change, actively seeks out opportunities, and cultivates resilience in the face of adversity. By nurturing specific traits and implementing effective strategies, entrepreneurs can foster a growth mindset that propels them on their entrepreneurial journey.

Let's now delve into the essential steps to cultivate an entrepreneurial growth mindset:

- Embrace a "Can-Do" Attitude

One of the significant steps in developing an entrepreneurial growth mindset is cultivating an optimistic attitude. Have faith in your capacity to learn, adapt, and overcome obstacles. Replace any self-doubt with self-assurance and approach every situation with the mindset that you can find solutions or gain valuable insights from it.

- Adopt a Growth-Oriented Perspective

Accept that work, practice, and learning can help you improve your abilities, skills, and intelligence. Emphasize the process of growth rather than focusing solely on immediate outcomes. View failures and setbacks as opportunities for learning and improvement rather than signs of defeat.

- Embrace Change and Uncertainty

Recognize that change is a constant in entrepreneurship and be open to embracing new ideas, technologies, and approaches. Develop a willingness to step outside your comfort zone and take calculated risks. Innovative ideas and fresh opportunities might result from embracing uncertainty and viewing it as a chance for development.

- Cultivate a Curious and Learning Mindset

Be observant of your surroundings and actively look for new information and perspectives. Embrace a mindset of continuous learning and improvement. Stay updated on industry trends, attend conferences and workshops, read books and articles, and seek out mentors and experts who can provide guidance and knowledge.

- Develop Resilience and Perseverance

The path of entrepreneurship is paved with ups, downs, and unavoidable setbacks. Develop resilience by bouncing back from failures, learning from them, and persevering in the face of challenges. View obstacles as temporary roadblocks that can be overcome with determination and creative problem-solving.

- Seek Feedback and Learn from Others

Actively seek feedback from mentors, peers, customers, and employees. Embrace constructive criticism and view it as a valuable chance for personal development and growth. Foster a supportive network of individuals who can offer guidance, advice, and diverse perspectives to help you along your journey.

- Set Goals and Take Action

Establish clear and meaningful goals that align with your vision and values. Construct a clear plan to achieve your goals by breaking them down into manageable chunks. Consistently take focused action towards your objectives while remaining adaptable and open to refining your approach. Remember to celebrate your accomplishments throughout the journey to keep your motivation and momentum high.

- Practice Self-Care

Maintain a growth mindset for your physical, mental, and emotional welfare. Prioritize self-care activities such as exercise, proper nutrition, rest, relaxation, and stress management. A healthy and balanced lifestyle supports clarity of thought, creativity, and well-being.

- Cultivate a Supportive Network

Associate with people who share your passion for entrepreneurship and are like-minded. Join networking groups, attend industry events, and seek out mentorship opportunities. Engage in meaningful conversations, share experiences, and learn from others who have successfully developed entrepreneurial careers.

- Reflect and Celebrate Progress

Regularly reflect on your journey, acknowledging your progress and how far you've come. Celebrate your achievements and milestones, no matter how small, as they serve as reminders of your growth and motivate you to keep moving forward.

Embracing an entrepreneurial growth mindset is not a destination but a journey. Self-improvement and personal development are ongoing processes. Remain focused and driven to see things through as you move forward.

Overcoming Limiting Beliefs And Negative Self-Talk

Entrepreneurship presents a path filled with obstacles that challenge our pursuit of goals. These obstacles often take the shape of limiting beliefs, which can undermine our progress and impede our success. Limiting beliefs and negative self-talk create self-imposed obstacles, convincing us that we lack the capability, worth, or entitlement to achieve our aspirations. As a result, they hindered our willingness to take the crucial actions and calculated risks required to flourish in the entrepreneurial domain.

How do we overcome limiting beliefs and negative self-talk?

Recognizing the existence of these barriers is the initial stride toward conquering them. Understanding that these beliefs are ingrained in every individual to varying degrees is crucial, as they can influence every facet of our lives, including our entrepreneurial endeavors. Understanding that these limiting beliefs are not grounded in reality but are instead a result of our subconscious mind and conditioning is crucial.

Limiting beliefs are strongly influenced by the conscious mind, which has a tendency to resist change and seek comfort in the familiar. It bombards us with thoughts such as "You can't do it," "You will fail," or "You are not good enough." These negative thoughts act as formidable roadblocks, impeding our progress and preventing us from taking the necessary actions to achieve our goals. They have a stifling effect on our entrepreneurial potential and must be overcome to unlock our true capabilities.

To transcend these self-imposed limitations and attain entrepreneurial success, it is essential to silence our conscious mind and harness the potential of our subconscious. Unlike the conscious mind, the subconscious is receptive to all thoughts without distinguishing between positive and negative. It responds to the instructions we provide, shaped by our beliefs, emotions, and aspirations. By consciously directing our subconscious towards positive and empowering thoughts, we can reshape our beliefs and pave the way for entrepreneurial triumph.

We can rewire our subconscious mind to align with our goals by shifting our negative self-talk to positive affirmations. With intentional focus, we can swap limiting beliefs for empowering ones. We must have faith in our capabilities and acknowledge our worthiness of success. Utilizing affirmations like "I have the ability," "I am worthy of success," and "I can conquer any obstacle" aids in reshaping our mindset and dismantling self-imposed barriers.

Furthermore, incorporating techniques like visualization and meditation can assist in rewiring our subconscious mind. Through visualization, we can vividly imagine our desired outcomes and immerse ourselves in the emotions linked to success. This practice deeply imprints our subconscious, making engaging in the actions required for goal attainment easier. By practicing meditation, we can quiet the conscious mind and access our inner wisdom and intuition, invaluable resources that can steer us toward entrepreneurial triumph.

Conquering limiting beliefs is a perpetual undertaking, necessitating unwavering dedication, introspection, and a readiness to question our assumptions and thinking patterns. Enveloping ourselves in a network of supportive individuals who share our aspirations can provide the motivation and inspiration for persisting through arduous circumstances. Recognizing that this process is not a singular event but an enduring personal development journey is key.

Recognizing and overcoming limiting beliefs is pivotal to attaining entrepreneurial success. By understanding the influence of our conscious and subconscious minds, we can seize command of our thoughts and beliefs, reshaping them into empowering forces that propel us along our entrepreneurial path. By nurturing a positive mindset and surmounting self-imposed constraints, we unlock the potential to achieve remarkable business triumphs and manifest the life we envision. This transformative journey paves the way for embracing boundless possibilities and realizing our true potential.

Time Management Skills for Business Owners

For entrepreneurs, establishing a harmonious equilibrium between work and personal life is of utmost importance. This balance not only enhances productivity but also facilitates personal growth. Managing your time effectively to nurture your business and personal well-being can be challenging. While tending to your personal life is vital for overall happiness, it is equally crucial to dedicate ample time and energy to your business to ensure its success.

Mastering the art of effective time management is crucial to establishing a harmonious work-life balance. To align the time you invest in your business with your personal life, consider implementing the following strategies:

❖ Harness technology for productivity

Operating a business in the digital age presents challenges and opportunities. The key lies in how effectively you leverage the available technology. Social media platforms can serve as valuable business tools but can be distracting and time-consuming. To ensure productivity, it is crucial to exercise self-discipline. Utilize your smartphone and other devices wisely, avoiding getting lost in the time-consuming realms of Twitter and Facebook.

Instead, employ technology to streamline your business operations. Take advantage of project management software, communication tools, and automation systems that can enhance efficiency and collaboration. These technologies enable you to stay organized, communicate effectively with your team, and automate repetitive tasks, freeing valuable time for more important responsibilities.

❖ Efficient Work Practices

Optimize your work practices to maximize productivity. Minimize distractions, create a dedicated workspace, and employ productivity techniques or group similar tasks. These strategies enable you to accomplish more in less time, leaving room for personal activities.

❖ Establish Boundaries

Recognize the importance of setting boundaries to protect your time and maintain productivity as a business owner. While being accessible to employees and customers is important, constantly overextending yourself can hinder your progress. Embrace using a "Do Not Disturb" sign when necessary to create focused work periods and boost your productivity. This practice is applicable not only to traditional workplaces but also to business owners who may face additional interruptions and requests.

❖ Embrace Delegation and Outsourcing

One of the keys to achieving a harmonious work-life balance is recognizing that you cannot do everything by yourself. As a business owner, delegating tasks others can effectively handle is crucial. This can be accomplished through hiring employees, outsourcing certain functions, or utilizing automation tools.

Delegating tasks allows you to distribute the workload and focus on high-priority responsibilities that require your expertise and attention. By entrusting competent individuals or external professionals with specific tasks, you lighten your workload and create opportunities for personal time and activities outside of work.

❖ Respect Appointments

In entrepreneurs' busy lives, allowing appointments and meetings to extend past their allotted time slots is easy. However, it's essential to recognize the value of your time and the importance of respecting both your schedule and that of others. Making a deliberate endeavor to abide by the designated timeframe for an appointment strictly is of significant importance.

Respecting the designated appointment time demonstrates professionalism and consideration for others and helps maintain a productive and efficient workflow. Honoring your commitments and adhering to the agreed-upon schedule create a positive reputation for reliability and time management.

Within the broader context of life, time represents a limited resource, and how we handle our daily tasks, meticulously accounting for each hour, profoundly influences our overall achievements. To reach higher levels of success, the cultivation of efficient time management abilities becomes indispensable. By optimizing how we allocate and prioritize our time, we can maximize productivity, seize opportunities, and accomplish our goals. Time management is the key to unlocking our full potential and achieving the level of success we aspire to. So, let's make it a priority to master the art of managing our time effectively and reap the rewards that come with it.

SERIES TEN
CHALLENGES AND
RESILIENCE

In pursuing success in business and life, individuals must preserve their energy, creativity, and passion despite the continuous presence of change, stress, and competition. Today, in a world where information overload is prevalent, it has become crucial to maintain this drive and enthusiasm while also achieving a harmonious work-life balance for personal growth and overall well-being. The constant influx of information adds to the complexity of our lives, and the current working environments impose higher levels of accountability and greater expectations compared to the past decade. Prioritizing self-care and finding equilibrium is essential in navigating these challenges effectively.

In today's context, resilience holds tremendous significance, be it on an individual or organizational level. As described by Webster's Dictionary, resilience is the ability to overcome hardship or adapt to changing circumstances. It involves the capacity to persist in the face of initial failures, navigate ambiguity and uncertainty, overcome obstacles and barriers, and sustainably envision the future. Mike Jay, the author of CPR for the Soul and Founder of Leadership University, emphasizes cultivating resilience in our lives and endeavors.

Renowned psychologist Albert Bandura highlights the unique capabilities inherent in human beings that profoundly influence our human experience. These capabilities encompass the ability to learn from our mistakes, envision the future, self-reflect, and effectively manage our emotions. They give us the tools to shape our destinies and maintain resilience in changing circumstances. Developing these innate qualities is crucial for bolstering our resilience, as they define our humanity. While other species lack the capacity for planning, self-reflection, and emotional management, these distinct attributes that make us human also serve as the bedrock for resilience during difficult times.

Entrepreneurship, widely recognized as an exciting and ever-evolving voyage, is undeniably accompanied by its trials. The pursuit of success rarely follows a straight trajectory, necessitating entrepreneurs to maneuver through diverse obstacles adeptly. These challenges serve as litmus tests for their perseverance, unwavering commitment, and adaptation capacity. Yet, resilience empowers entrepreneurs to surmount these hurdles, emerging fortified and triumphantly realizing their objectives.

This comprehensive series will delve into the integral connection between challenges, resilience, and entrepreneurial success. Our exploration will encompass a range of common obstacles entrepreneurs encounter, offering invaluable insights and strategies to conquer them. By embracing the transformative potential of resilience, entrepreneurs can cultivate the mental strength required to endure and flourish amid adversity.

Elements Of Resilience

1. Embrace things as they are not as you hope or wish they would be

During difficult periods, the instinct to deny reality may arise as a means of self-preservation. Yet, genuine readiness and personal development can only emerge when we courageously confront the truth. Denial merely prolongs adversity and obstructs advancement. With each passing day and month that we evade reality, the repercussions intensify.

Nurturing resilience, whether as individuals or organizations, necessitates releasing wishful thinking and avoiding dwelling on the past. Instead, we must confront the present and future with bravery. Resilience entails foreseeing and embracing change before it becomes imperative. It involves actively preparing for the future rather than passively accepting our circumstances. By embracing reality and taking proactive measures, we can establish a strong resilience foundation and effectively navigate our challenges.

2. Prioritize what truly matters and navigate accordingly.

When we need clarity regarding our priorities, our actions and behaviors become aimless, hindering our resilience. Strong values act as compasses, guiding our decisions and actions. During times of crisis and adversity, this clarity becomes even more crucial, enabling us to navigate through uncertainty. With a map or clear guidance, the recovery path becomes more manageable. Successful individuals and organizations possess strong values that steer their behavior during difficult times, helping them stay on track and bounce back effectively. By anchoring ourselves in our core values, we can align our actions with what truly matters, enhancing our resilience and facilitating our ability to overcome obstacles.

3. Embrace and find purpose in life's circumstances.

Our capacity to bounce back from adversity is fundamentally dependent on resilience. If we spend time complaining and lamenting our challenges, we hinder our capacity to reflect upon and learn from these difficulties. Resilient individuals and organizations possess the ability to uncover hidden opportunities amidst adversity. They bridge the wisdom gained from past experiences to the present innovation, paving the way toward a brighter future. By accepting the circumstances and seeking meaning, we empower ourselves to move beyond setbacks and transform challenges into stepping stones for growth and development.

4. Know yourself

Knowing our strengths and limitations will help us exploit and control our deficiencies better. When we spend much time operating out of our weaknesses, more effort is expended, and results are dispersed. Directing our actions around our strengths allows us to be more efficient and effective in freeing creative energy. Problems and challenges will not be transcended if we become victims of blind spots and minimize our talents and creativity.

Common Challenges Entrepreneurs Face And Solutions

Embarking on the entrepreneurial path entails a voyage brimming with exhilaration, ambition, and the pursuit of achievement. Nonetheless, it also presents a considerable array of obstacles to overcome. Entrepreneurship requires individuals to navigate through a myriad of obstacles and hurdles that can test their resilience, determination, and ability to adapt. Understanding and effectively addressing these challenges are crucial for entrepreneurial success. Let's explore some common challenges entrepreneurs face and provide practical strategies to overcome them, ensuring a smoother path toward achieving your goals.

1. Uncertainty and Risk

One of the inherent challenges of entrepreneurship is dealing with uncertainty and taking calculated risks. Starting a business entails venturing into the unknown, with uncertain outcomes and inevitable risks. To overcome this challenge, entrepreneurs should focus on the following:

a. Market Research: Conduct thorough market research to gain insights into customer needs, competition, and market trends. This helps in making informed decisions and minimizing risks.

b. Planning and Analysis: Develop a well-thought-out business plan that outlines goals, strategies, and contingencies. Regularly analyze and adapt the plan based on market feedback and changing circumstances.

c. Embrace Failure as Learning: View failures as valuable learning opportunities rather than setbacks. Adopt a growth mindset that embraces experimentation, iteration, and continuous improvement.

2. Financial Management

Managing finances is another common challenge for entrepreneurs, especially in the beginning. Limited capital, cash flow management, and securing funding can be daunting. Overcoming financial challenges involves:

a. Budgeting and Forecasting: Develop a comprehensive budget and financial forecast to track expenses, manage cash flow, and anticipate future financial needs. Seek professional advice when necessary.

b. Seeking Funding Options: Explore various funding sources such as loans, grants, crowdfunding, or angel investors. Prepare a solid business plan and compelling pitch to attract potential investors.

c. Cost Optimization: Continuously evaluate and optimize expenses without compromising quality. Look for opportunities to reduce overhead costs, negotiate better deals with suppliers, and explore cost-effective alternatives.

3. Time Management

Entrepreneurs often face the daunting task of managing multiple responsibilities within limited time frames. To effectively manage time and increase productivity:

a. Prioritize Tasks: Identify high-priority tasks that align with business goals and focus on completing them first. Delegate or outsource non-essential tasks to free up time for critical activities.

b. Time Blocking: Utilize time-blocking techniques to allocate specific time slots for different activities. This helps create structure and ensures dedicated time for important tasks.

c. Avoid Procrastination: Develop discipline and overcome procrastination by breaking tasks into smaller, manageable steps. Set realistic deadlines and hold yourself accountable.

4. Building a Strong Team

Entrepreneurs often face challenges in building and managing a competent team. Finding the right talent, fostering a positive work culture, and delegating effectively is crucial for long-term success. To overcome this challenge:

a. Hiring Process: Implement a strategic hiring process that includes screening, interviewing, and assessing candidates based on their skills, experience, and cultural fit. Spend some time selecting the best people for your team.

b. Effective Communication: Establish open and transparent communication channels within the team. Communicate expectations, provide feedback, and encourage collaboration.

c. Continuous Development: Invest in the professional development of your team members through training programs, mentorship, and growth opportunities. This cultivates a motivated and skilled workforce.

5. Work-Life Balance

Entrepreneurs often find it challenging to balance work and personal life. Neglecting personal well-being can lead to burnout and hinder long-term success. To maintain a healthy work-life balance:

a. Set Boundaries: Establish clear boundaries between work and personal life. Designate specific time slots for work and prioritize personal activities, hobbies, and self-care.

b. Delegate and Outsource: Delegate tasks that can be handled by others, whether through hiring employees, outsourcing certain functions, or leveraging automation tools. This frees up time for personal endeavors.

c. Time for Reflection: Dedicate time for self-reflection and relaxation. Engage in rejuvenating activities for your body and mind, such as hobby pursuit, exercise, or meditation.

Entrepreneurship is a journey that requires individuals to overcome various challenges to achieve their goals. By acknowledging and addressing these common obstacles, entrepreneurs can enhance their chances of success. Remember, challenges are not roadblocks but opportunities for growth and learning. Embrace these challenges proactively and utilize the strategies and techniques discussed to overcome them.

Resistance To Adversity And Perseverance In It

Life presents us with numerous challenges and setbacks that put our strength and determination to the test. When confronted with adversity, our resilience and perseverance empower us to bounce back, evolve, and ultimately triumph. Resilience entails enduring and recovering from difficult circumstances, while perseverance involves unwavering dedication and persistence in the pursuit of our goals despite obstacles. Together, these attributes create a formidable synergy that enables individuals to conquer adversity and attain personal and professional success.

Understanding Resilience

Resilience is not innate; it can be cultivated and developed over time. It involves adapting to and bouncing back from adversity, setbacks, and challenges. Here are some key aspects of resilience:

a. Positive Mindset: Resilient individuals maintain a positive outlook even in difficult situations. They have confidence in their capacity to overcome challenges and see failures as chances to grow.

b. Emotional Regulation: Resilient individuals effectively manage their emotions and stress levels. They develop healthy coping mechanisms and seek support when needed.

c. Problem-solving Skills: Resilience involves identifying solutions and proactively addressing challenges. Resilient individuals approach problems with a solution-oriented mindset.

The Power of Perseverance

Perseverance is the unwavering commitment to achieving one's goals despite obstacles, failures, or discouragement. It is the resolute determination to persevere, even in the face of adversities or setbacks. Here are some key aspects of perseverance:

a. Clear Vision and Goals: Perseverance requires clearly understanding one's vision and goals. Setting specific, measurable, attainable, relevant, and time-bound goals provides a roadmap for progress and helps maintain focus.

b. Grit and Determination: Perseverance involves staying dedicated and committed to the desired outcome, even when faced with challenges or temptations to give up. It requires mental toughness and a willingness to put in the necessary effort.

c. Adaptability: Perseverance is not about stubbornly sticking to a single approach. It also involves being adaptable and open to adjusting strategies when necessary. Flexibility allows for learning from failures and finding alternative paths to success.

Strategies for Developing Resilience and Perseverance

a. Cultivate a Growth Mindset: Embrace the belief that effort and practice can develop abilities and skills. Adopting a growth mindset allows you to view challenges as opportunities for growth and learning.

b. Build a Supportive Network: Surround yourself with positive and supportive individuals who can provide encouragement, guidance, and practical assistance when needed. Seek mentors or join communities of like-minded individuals.

c. Practice Self-Care: Take care of your physical, emotional, and mental well-being. Set aside time for activities like exercise, meditation, time in nature, or hobbies that will help you to feel refreshed and renewed.

d. Set Realistic Goals: Break down your goals into smaller, manageable steps. Celebrate milestones along the way to stay motivated and build momentum. Remem that growth is not always straight-linear and that setbacks are inevitable on the way.

e. Learn from Setbacks: Instead of dwelling on failures, view them as opportunities for learning and growth. Reflect on what went wrong, identify lessons, and use them to refine your approach and make better decisions in the future.

f. Seek Inspiration: Read about people who overcame challenges and accomplished wonderful things. Their stories can provide inspiration, motivation, and valuable insights into overcoming challenges.

The resilient people of today and tomorrow are the ones who can face reality head-on, knowing what's important at the moment, leveraging their strengths, and making meaning out of hardships. We create the future through our response to the challenges of today.

Resilience and perseverance are essential qualities that enable individuals to overcome adversity and achieve personal and professional success. Individuals can more easily and successfully navigate through the ups and downs of life by establishing resilience and perseverance.

Staying Motivated And Focused

Intelligence and physical prowess are not the only factors influencing success in life. Instead, individuals with an unyielding determination often achieve the greatest accomplishments, even in the most challenging circumstances. Winston Churchill recognized that persistent and unwavering effort, rather than inherent strength or intelligence, unlocks our true potential.

Consistency in practice is undeniably the key to success in most endeavors. However, putting this principle into action is often more challenging than it sounds. Various factors can disrupt our focus and commitment. Life's unexpected events, distractions, boredom, and the lack of noticeable progress can easily demoralize us.

Maintaining motivation and focus can be challenging, mainly when negative thoughts about the future and feelings of sadness arise. These emotions are often triggered by physical discomfort, significant life distractions, or a lack of clear goals to pursue and anticipate. However, key elements can assist in establishing goals and finding sources of motivation.

Negativity is a fluctuating experience influenced by the level of mental training we provide. It resembles a cycle of highs and lows, and the remedy lies in training our minds with positive reinforcements. By cultivating a positive mindset, we can sustain motivation and progress continually.

- The process typically begins with identifying your wants or needs.
- From there, you engage in theoretical thinking or imagination to explore potential solutions.
- Convert these solutions into practical and workable ideas.
- Subsequently, you analyze and select the ideas that are feasible and attainable.

- With achievable plans in place, you can envision the desired outcome.
- This vision inspires, fueling your imagination and planning to manifest it.
- As the inspiration intensifies, it ignites motivation, compelling you to take specific actions toward materializing your envisioned ideas and goals.

While you may occasionally veer off track, maintaining focus on your goals and nurturing your burning desire to achieve them will eventually steer you back in the right direction. This occurs when pursuing a long-term goal and striving to accomplish it within a limited timeframe. Long-term goals may provide little motivation and focus, as the results often require materializing time. A straightforward remedy is to pursue short-term goals instead, enabling faster achievements. Additionally, it is vital to celebrate each accomplishment to acknowledge progress and perpetuate your motivation. This celebration serves to keep your motivation burning brightly.

Upon reaching a goal, it is important not to halt and become complacent. Instead, strive to create a fresh vision or set a new goal. Consider your next destination and how you want to use your time to get there. This approach will maintain your inspiration and motivation, propelling you to persevere through the tasks and obstacles on your path to success.

More than merely expressing your desire to achieve something is required. Many individuals talk about their aspirations, but only some follow through or take the necessary steps to attain them. Remember, your desired goals will not materialize on their own; you must invest the effort to make them a reality. To do so, having a crystal-clear vision of what you truly want is crucial. This vision should be so vivid that you can envision yourself feeling and experiencing it as if you already possess it. This clarity and sense of immediacy will be the driving force that propels you to strive harder—elements necessary for success.

Training your mind to adopt the right mindset is essential for staying motivated and focused on achieving success. By cultivating the right mindset, you can effectively expand your business.

Tips For Bouncing Back From Failures And Setbacks

Setbacks are an inevitable part of life's journey. We all face moments of adversity, from small stumbles to major setbacks that can make us feel like we've hit rock bottom. Failures come in different shapes and sizes, whether losing a game, missing out on a promotion, or dealing with losing a loved one. The truth is only some have the natural ability to navigate these emotional storms with ease. Some people possess remarkable resilience, bouncing back from setbacks, dusting themselves off, and courageously embracing new beginnings.

The entrepreneurial journey is comparable to a thrilling rollercoaster ride filled with exhilarating highs and challenging lows. In this ever-changing landscape, triumph and failure intertwine, pushing our resilience to its limits. Setbacks are intrinsic to the entrepreneurial path, but how we react to these obstacles determines our character and future accomplishments.

Entrepreneurial setbacks can come in various shapes and sizes, such as underperforming product launches, ineffective marketing strategies, or financial challenges that strain your business. Nevertheless, by cultivating the right mindset and employing effective strategies, you can rebound from these setbacks and propel yourself toward fresh opportunities. To navigate and conquer entrepreneurial setbacks, consider implementing the following key approaches:

1. Reframe your Perspective

Reframing the situation is important when faced with a setback in your business. This doesn't involve dwelling on it or replaying the events repeatedly in your mind. Instead, it's about adopting a new perspective that allows you to move forward. Remember, dwelling on negative emotions only keeps you stagnant. Reframing is not about denying failure or applying a superficial positive thinking approach.

One effective approach is consciously creating distance between yourself and the setback. Allow yourself a moment of reflection on the situation, consciously redirecting your attention from the emotions you have experienced to gain a deeper understanding of the underlying causes behind those feelings. Imagine if the same situation happened to someone else, allowing yourself to gain a fresh perspective and prevent getting caught up in the intense emotions of the moment. By mentally stepping back, you can better manage your emotions and understand your reactions. For instance, observing a painting from a distance makes the bigger picture clearer. As a result, you'll be able to evaluate the situations and feelings with more objectivity.

2. Embrace positive mindset

Bouncing back from setbacks involves dedicating time to contemplate and engage in activities that genuinely bring you happiness. Seek experiences that fully immerse you on all levels, allowing you to enter a flow state. Engage in activities that amplify your sense of fulfillment, involvement, and joy. It's crucial to prioritize activities that bring happiness to you personally rather than conforming to what others find fulfilling. Remember, this is about discovering and nurturing your unique sources of happiness and fulfillment rather than striving to meet societal expectations.

3. Pay attention to what you missed.

Understanding the factors that led to your failure not only provides a sense of clarity but also empowers you to address your contributions to the outcome. Reflect on any details or signals you may have missed, giving you a false sense of being on the right track. Consider whether you were overly focused on positive indicators, such as compliments from your boss or temporary moments of calm in a relationship, causing you to overlook significant critiques about your work ethic or the growing distance between you and your partner. By acknowledging and learning from these missed cues, you can gain valuable insights for personal growth and future success.

4. Embrace the Power of Action and Perseverance

Resilience extends beyond mere recovery; it encompasses the proactive pursuit of solutions and unwavering perseverance when confronted with challenges in business.

By embracing a growth mindset, learning from setbacks, building resilience, and taking decisive action, you can transform entrepreneurial setbacks into opportunities for growth and ultimate success. Remember, setbacks are not the end of your journey—they are merely detours that can lead to new and exciting paths. Stay resilient, remain adaptable, and keep forging ahead with passion and determination.

Conclusion

The entrepreneurship journey is complex and demanding, filled with numerous challenges and obstacles. Throughout my exploration of empowering strategies for success, valuable insights have been uncovered to guide aspiring and seasoned entrepreneurs on their quest.

One key takeaway is the importance of resilience and adaptability in adversity. Entrepreneurship is not for the faint-hearted, and setbacks are inevitable. However, by maintaining a strong sense of resilience and embracing failures as learning opportunities, entrepreneurs can rise above challenges and propel themselves toward success.

Strategic planning is another vital aspect that must be considered. Setting clear goals, formulating actionable plans and regularly evaluating and adjusting strategies are essential for long-term success. Market research, competitor analysis, and staying attuned to industry trends enable entrepreneurs to stay ahead of the curve and seize new opportunities.

Building a strong network and cultivating meaningful relationships is crucial for entrepreneurial growth. Surrounding oneself with a supportive community and seeking mentorship can provide guidance, collaboration, and access to valuable resources. Digital platforms offer endless possibilities for expanding networks and connecting with like-minded individuals.

The impact of technology on entrepreneurship must be considered. Leveraging digital tools and platforms enables entrepreneurs to streamline operations, enhance productivity, and reach a wider audience. Utilizing social media for effective marketing and branding, harnessing data analytics for informed decision-making, and embracing emerging technologies drive innovation and growth.

Maintaining personal well-being and a healthy work-life balance is essential for long-term success. Neglecting self-care can lead to burnout and hinder overall performance. Strategies for stress management, prioritizing self-care, and nurturing personal relationships are vital for sustaining energy, creativity, and passion throughout the entrepreneurial journey.

In entrepreneurship, audacity and perseverance are of great importance. Embracing the challenges, uncertainties, and setbacks is part of the journey. With each hurdle overcome, entrepreneurs become more resilient and resourceful, paving the way for growth and success.

Remember that entrepreneurship continuously pursues growth, innovation, and impact. By implementing the empowering strategies explored, entrepreneurs can unlock their full potential, overcome challenges, and create a lasting legacy.

On this entrepreneurial journey, there are no guarantees, but with the right mindset, strategic planning, a supportive network, and a commitment to personal well-being, the possibilities are endless. So, let us embark on our entrepreneurial journeys with unwavering determination and an unyielding spirit, creating a future marked by success, fulfillment, and realizing our dreams.

www.ingramcontent.com/pod-product-compliance
Lightning Source LLC
Chambersburg PA
CBHW070120010626
45794CB00012B/359